Rising From The Ashes

Disaster Recovery for the Homeowner

Other Books by Fran Rutherford

Questions for the Thinker™ Study Guides:
Greek Classics
Ancient Rome
Old World Europe

Fran has written a Must Have guide on how to proceed following a disaster that has destroyed or seriously damaged your home and its contents. She has laid out a plan, lists, insurance information and resources that would have been immeasurable help to us when we suffered a catastrophic loss to fire several years ago. Thank you, Fran, for helping so many people get back on their feet and through your encouragement 'move forward'. Helene Forster

Rising from the Ashes
disasterrecoverybook.com
qthinker@q.com
719-229-2875

ww   .com

ii

Rising From The Ashes

Disaster Recovery for the Homeowner

Fran Rutherford

Aquinas and More Publishing
Ft. Collins, CO

Cover Image *of Rebekah Delgado surveying the destruction caused by the fire.*

Back Cover Image *of the initial clean-up crew.* *From left to right:* *Kelly Collins, Richard Gastellum, Breánne Rutherford, James Rutherford, Paula Rutherford, Ian Rutherford, Rebekah Delgado, Larry Rutherford, Fran Rutherford and Michael Rutherford*

Inset Picture of author taken at Molls Gap, County Kerry, Ireland

Cover Design by Larry Rutherford

ISBN-13: 978-0-9994131-1-1
ISBN-10: 0-9994131-1-2

Dedication

Our recovery from the Black Forest Fire of 2013 would have been possible but more difficult without the determined efforts of my husband, Larry. He put to good use all the training and practice of a lifetime career as a logistics planner in the Air Force. He was determined that the fire would not rob us of our life and that we wouldn't waste any time in our efforts to reclaim our home. So with fortitude and focus, he managed the entire recovery.

I am so grateful for his foresight, his quiet strength, and the good ideas he had for making our house beautiful. His modus operandi is **"you've got to have a plan."** He came up with a plan and in 14 months his plan flourished into our re-establishment at Casa Colorada. I love you, Larry.

Contents

Foreword

In 2013, Black Forest was hit with the most destructive fire in Colorado history in which around 500 homes were destroyed. We were away and no one was allowed to go in to take a few things we wanted to save. A phone call from our daughter confirmed that our house was among those lost, as our son had seen an aerial shot of our property taken by local news media. Not only did the fire take our house, but it took our barn, our greenhouse, five acres of ponderosa trees and all our belongings.

We were stunned. Far away from home in Alaska, we could do nothing but wait till we returned home to let the reality of what had happened sink in. We loved our home. It told our story of 43 years together, in the way it was decorated, by the things we owned, and with all the memorabilia that put our signature upon it. It held many wonderful memories for us and for our family, both immediate and extended, and for the many grandchildren we have. We had recently hosted a family reunion for 32 people and the sweetness of that wonderful time lingered on. And then, the fire hit.

I wish I could say we did everything right in the restoration of our home and life. We didn't even do everything that is in this book! Though we did most of it, there were things we learned later that we wish we had known to do when we were in the process, and I have included those here.

This handbook is written for you homeowners who endure a destruction of **real property**** in the hope that you will find clear guidance in your own reconstruction. Since we have first-hand knowledge of such a loss, we want to share our experience not only of that loss, but more importantly, of recovery. We hope you will benefit from what we learned and restore your life as quickly and efficiently as you can. It isn't an easy road and if even one family is helped by the information here, it will have been worth the time to put these suggestions and ideas to paper. It is also written as a help for all homeowners to take stock of what you have and to help you plan for an emergency, should it arrive down the road.

Rutherford Pines before the fire

***Insurance terms** used for the first time in this book are found in Appendix 1

Introduction

Getting over a painful experience is much like crossing the monkey bars. You have to let go at some point in order to move forward.
C. S. Lewis

One is never completely prepared for a natural disaster, but there are things that can be done "just in case." Later in this book, I will give you suggestions on steps you can take in advance, just in case some disaster like a tornado, flood, fire or hurricane should hit. A bit of pre-planning makes coping with a major catastrophe so much smoother. We always tried to be prepared for things to happen. We had set aside a bit of extra food and water, just in case, but when a fire or some other natural disaster hits, all that one has saved can be taken away in a flash. There were other things we should have done to be prepared which we learned about too late. So how were we to begin? Bits of information were available, but there was so much that it was difficult to know where to start. (What had to be done first, and when, were questions we had, but answers were not readily available). Our two computers had been incinerated with everything else, and thus, we didn't have ready access to the internet. So we blindly began what was to be a year-long recovery.

We spoke to a lot of people in the days, weeks and months following the fire and were struck by the different responses to this tragedy in their lives. Of course, everybody was initially devastated, ourselves included. It had been a dry year and we had been worrying about fires for months, so when the fire started on that afternoon of

June 11, 2013, it was not a total surprise. Almost exactly a year before, another large fire had hit the west side of our city and claimed 346 homes. So in May of 2013 we did major fire mitigation by cutting down trees and removing ladder fuel and anything that would pose a hazard to our home except for the tall trees which were part of the forest. We stacked the wood away from the house and thought everything was pretty safe. According to the standards for mitigation, our property was in compliance.

And then the fire storm came. The fire moved very quickly and created its own wind. Firebrands were carried over a mile to other parts of Black Forest, igniting new fires wherever they landed. The winds were shifting by the minute, and nobody was exempt from the possibility of being burned. Evacuations were begun and all but two people got out of the forest burn area. Some people evacuated their horses and other livestock while some had to leave them. There was little time for indecision or for action. The fire burned for days and it was a waiting game for everybody involved. The sheriff had a list of confirmed home losses which everybody watched anxiously, but not all the homes were listed, ours included, and it had burned within five hours of the onset of the fire.

Once the reality of the devastation set in, some people responded in disbelief; others in anger, thinking the firefighters should have done more to save their homes. Some were so overwhelmed that they couldn't move forward. Some had no insurance, so it truly represented a total loss in that they did not have the means to rebuild. Some moved away. Others dug in and made the decision to rebuild. We were in the last group and this book tells the story of how we did it.

Right after a disaster of this magnitude, help comes from all around—the *Red Cross, Catholic Charities*, numerous churches, the *Salvation Army, Samaritan's Purse* and other charitable groups. Individuals and people from various businesses and other organizations all appeared on the scene to help. In our case, an emergency response center was set up in the El Paso County Citizens Service Center and in addition to the utility companies, many groups were represented with various kinds of help to offer. We were given care packages, boxes of food, cleaning supplies, cosmetics and coupons to *Goodwill* for free clothing. The immediate needs of the fire victims were met. People could sign up for additional help with sifting through the ashes, removing trees and clearing property. Numerous church groups sent people to help. Quilters made quilts for all the now-homeless residents and a couple of organizations set up a Christmas giveaway of ornaments, trees, lights and other items associated with the holidays. So much energy and love poured forth from every corner! We were overwhelmed by the generosity and selflessness of total strangers ready to help us. Members of our family came from various states to help us with the cleanup and to help us plant new trees.

My husband Larry was a logistics planner during most of his Air Force career, so he immediately ditched his "retired" hat, put on his "planner's" hat and began our rebuild and the reconstruction of our lives. We were over two thousand miles from home, but that didn't slow him down. From memory, he quickly drew up some sketches of our house and then called an architectural designer who had done some work for us before and asked him to start drawing up house plans based on those sketches. We decided that we wanted to rebuild a house similar to the one we had lost because the parcel of land we were on did not allow for much change in the footprint due to the location of the well and septic system. Also, we loved our home and thought we would be better equipped to get on with our lives in something similar. He contacted our insurance company and got the process started for our **claim**, setting up a meeting with a Claim's **Adjuster** for the day we arrived home. The adjuster told us we would have to give the insurance company a list of everything we had lost. Let that sink in a moment. Do you know exactly what you own? We didn't either, but we had to start somewhere.

Being on a ship and then a train, we had many hours to brainstorm what needed to be done and to start listing everything we could remember owning. It gave us something to occupy our minds in the long hours into days before we could actually see the damage.

Our insurance policy provided for our immediate needs for housing, so we moved into a hotel the day we arrived and began looking for a house to rent during our rebuild. We were in the hotel for a month and then moved into a house for 11 months. Our insurance adjuster told us we had to be in our new house and have all our furnishings bought within a year if we wanted to collect the maximum allowed by our policy. Depending on insurance companies, that rule varied. Some people were actually told up front they had two years in which to rebuild. Even two years didn't sound like a lot of time, and we were only allowed half that!

Though several days had passed since the fire had started when we finally arrived back in Colorado, we were not allowed to immediately enter the burn area because of flare-ups and hot spots from the fire. Our children came from out of town to accompany us on our first visit to our burned out property. We were given three hours by the authorities to look over the area, during which time we came to grips with the magnitude of our loss, cried a lot, walked the five acres looking for something that might have escaped the blaze and reminisced about how wonderful it was before the fire. Then we began the arduous task of sifting through the ashes. Our first assessment was correct: we had lost everything we owned from our dwelling to just about everything in and around it.

Family members with us on our first entry back on the property

We simply couldn't believe that destruction from a fire could be so total. Officials reported that the heat reached around 2500 degrees F. It mangled steel, melted aluminum and glass, vaporized brass and pot metal. It also consumed all the vegetation around the house and property. The fire killed all the trees in its path and left behind a blanket of ash that worked its way into our shoes, clothing, hair and skin and probably our lungs as well, even though we wore masks as we worked in it.

Walking the burned property

A bit of a disclaimer

This is NOT a book focused on dealing with the emotional trauma which everybody endures to some degree in a disaster of this magnitude. I am not a psychologist or counselor, so if you need professional help, please seek it. I would just say, however, that you should be wary of anybody who encourages you to drag out your emotional recovery before you begin the long move forward, because you could quickly find yourself out of money and left with nothing. Also, moving forward is, in itself, a form of positive therapy.

First Things

*Put first things first and second things are thrown
in. Put second things first and you lose both first
and second things.*
C. S. Lewis

Notifying Family/Friends

I would suggest that the first thing you do is notify
your family that you are OK. The anxiety caused by not
knowing the fate of loved ones is unsettling, and it is a
good idea to let others know your whereabouts and
condition as soon as possible. That being said, since you
are traumatized by this event, ask your family or closest
friends to notify others so you don't spend your energy
calling everybody you know. If you use social media, that
may be the easiest way to let "the crowd" know how you
are doing. It may also be a vehicle for letting others know
your immediate needs and ways they can help. You will
possibly get plenty of offers of help but will be so
overwhelmed that you won't know how to respond.

Meeting with your Adjuster

Evaluating the damage is pretty straight forward. You
will need to meet with your insurance adjuster as quickly
as possible so that he can make the initial assessment and
authorize the start-up funds for your recovery. Our
experience and that of others who were covered by
different insurance companies was that we were
immediately provided with a partial payout of the value of

our homeowner's policy to begin rebuilding and refurnishing our home. We were also provided with a hotel to stay in and instructed to keep all our receipts for food, laundry, etc. to file with them at a later date. At that first meeting with your adjuster, be sure to go over the details of exactly what is covered by your policy so that you know what kind of help to expect in the coming days and months. Since you may have lost everything, you likely won't have a copy of your policy, so be sure to ask him for a copy of it. There may be provisions in your policy that you had never thought about or realized were there, yet you have been paying for them, so be thorough in reviewing it. For instance, we had a provision in our policy that covered the removal of debris. Not every policy has that, and when you are talking about the materials in the house itself and the contents, the cost to remove it all can be prohibitive. You will be dealing with your adjuster often in the coming weeks, so it is important to have a good rapport with him and a sense of trust.

Trust and rapport with your adjuster are essential

A word to the wise

Don't be fooled by what will seem like a huge amount of money when your adjuster hands you a couple of large checks to get started on your recovery. Most of us have never held a check for $100,000 or more and you may think it is a lot of cash. However, expenses mount up very quickly and there is usually a string attached to those checks. (If you have a mortgage, one of them actually has to go to your lender). The other check will be your start-up funds for replacing contents. Your insurance company may require receipts and a complete list of your home's contents before they give you the remainder of your money. They will also be monitoring your rebuild and paying out as the construction moves forward. So you must be frugal and proceed carefully.

Housing

You will need a place to stay while you reconstruct your life. During the initial days you may be fortunate enough to have friends and family to stay with, but in our mobile society, that isn't always the case. Oftentimes temporary shelters are set up following large-scale disasters, and they may be your only option for the immediate future. It is important to discuss the provisions of your homeowner's insurance policy with your adjuster because many policies provide for immediate and sometimes long-term housing while you rebuild. In our case, since the policy provided for housing, the person within the insurance company whose job it was to arrange housing took care of all the details and we didn't have to negotiate either the hotel we would be in temporarily or the house where we would live for the eleven months it took us to rebuild. Some people were told to secure their own housing and the insurance company would reimburse them if they saved the receipts. That is not a desirable way to go because it uses up a lot of cash up front, so you want the company to handle the arrangements if possible. We found that all the companies had different ways of handling housing, so it will be important to discuss this with your particular adjuster.

Temporary housing should be more or less comparable to what has been lost

Property Attention

Securing Remaining Possessions

It is undisputed that a disaster not only brings out the best in people, but also the worst in others. For that reason, it is understandable that you will want to account for your home and possessions as quickly as possible. Floods, tornadoes and hurricanes, as well as fires and earthquakes can wreak various amounts of havoc, from minimal damage to total destruction. Some homes may require repairs while others may need to be totally rebuilt. Some possessions may be intact while others may need to be hauled to the landfill because they are completely destroyed. You and your insurance adjuster have to make those judgements.

If you have the opportunity to return to your home, you should make every effort to find and secure valuable possessions as soon as possible. Even though there may be local law enforcement on the scene and possibly the National Guard, looters always seem to appear out of nowhere to prey on the victims of catastrophic events, and they look for items they can sell or use themselves. They also look for financial records, credit cards, and bank information. On top of everything else

Larry explaining the clean-up plan to our daughters-in-law, Paula and Breánne

you are dealing with, you don't want to have to deal with fraud perpetrated against you because someone has gotten hold of your personal and financial information. I have created a checklist of things you may want to look for first in the event there is anything left. (See Appendix 4)

Treasure Hunting

As hopeless at it may seem on first examination, it is worth looking for something that may have had meaning to you before the disaster. Almost always some things will survive and their importance to you shouldn't be underestimated.

As we approached our burned out property, one thing that was readily visible was a statue of the Blessed Virgin Mary. All the paint had been burned off the concrete statue, but it was still standing on the brick pedestal and served as a beacon for us. My niece, Andrea, came from Houston to restore the statue.

Concrete statue of the Blessed Virgin Mary

Author's niece, Andrea, restoring statue

Our youngest son asked me what he should look for as he was sifting ashes in the rubble that had been our home. I half kiddingly told him to see if he could find my wedding ring which I had left on a shelf in the bathroom. As unbelievable as it may seem, he found it! We took it to a local jeweler who cleaned it up and it looks as good as new. She said the diamond was a bit yellowed from the heat, but it was not visible to the naked eye.

Wedding ring found by our son, Mike

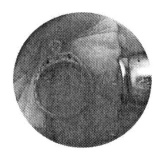

Our son, Mike, hunting for treasure

Our daughter found a ceramic Hopi Storyteller Figure which had been in the family for a number of years. Because of the high heat at which ceramics are fired, this piece managed to survive not only the fall from the first story into the basement, but also the high heat at which the fire burned.

Our daughter, Rebekah, with Hopi Storyteller Figure

We also found a china plate which was blackened but not broken or chipped. We were able to clean it up and it is almost as good as new. It is a poignant reminder of many gatherings we had in our home in the past.

Lenox China "Friends and Family" Plate

Our son, Ian, with a Russian teacup which survived intact

Crèche pieces found in the rubble by the author's brother, Richard

The other small items we found were pieces of charred pottery, a Russian teacup, and individual figures to various Christmas crèches which we now put together during the holidays as one composite crèche, reminding us that we can put ourselves back together with gratitude.

A friend came over with a huge tank full of water. He knew Larry was a gardener and perhaps would want to see if any little plants might have survived but were in need of water. Sure enough, the asparagus was coming back and various other little sprouts were seen popping up through the ash. We are sure they were very grateful for the water and we were very grateful for this unusual act of kindness.

10

Friend, John Erickson, arrived with a tank of water for Larry's garden

So many people helped in whatever way they could, and we were blessed with their creativity and generosity. Those acts of kindness meant so much to us and we will always be grateful. They have also provided us with ideas as to how we can help others should the need arise.

First Things Checklist

- ☐ Notify Family and Friends of your Whereabouts and Condition
- ☐ Meet with your Adjuster
- ☐ Arrange Housing
- ☐ Secure Remaining Possessions
- ☐ Hunt for Treasure

Secondary Details

Crying is all right in its own way while it lasts.
But you have to stop sooner or later, and then
you still have to decide what to do.
C. S. Lewis

Utilities

Telephone and Internet

Utilities are one of the last things to come to mind when you are facing a disaster, but they can't be ignored. We didn't think about this problem till much later and we assumed that the utility companies would automatically take care of what needed to be done. In our case, that didn't happen. Because we hadn't thought of using social media and our family didn't know all our friends, many people tried to call us to check on our condition. Since voicemail comes through the phone company and isn't tied to the physical phone, it continued to take messages, thus falsely reassuring our friends that our house must have miraculously escaped the inferno. When we finally realized that we were still being charged for phone and internet service we weren't using, we asked the phone company to temporarily suspend our service. They did so, but all our voicemails disappeared and we never did get back to all those people who called.

The other problem with the telephone became apparent much later when we tried to have the phone company come to the property to physically lay new phone lines. Since their customer service phone reps are often out of the country, they don't know about the circumstances affecting a particular area and they couldn't seem to understand that it wasn't just a matter of flipping a switch to restore service. They actually had to lay new line because any parts of the old line that hadn't burned up were dug up during the construction of the new house. It literally took months before we got that problem straightened up. That is one more reason why things can't be put off. You never know what glitches are going to happen to slow down your progress.

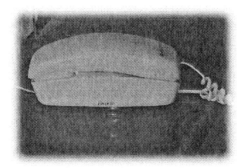

**Even in the digital age, some
people still use landline
telephones!**

Water and Sewer

We live in the country so we are responsible for our own water and septic. That means that we had to contact a well installer to come and not only inspect the well, but also to replace the well head which had burned off. He also put on a temporary faucet so water would be available for the contractors. In order to get water out of the well, however, we had to have a power source, so my husband purchased a generator. After that was done we had to take a water sample to the health department to make sure that the water was safe to drink. The contractor insisted that we have water available during the construction, so that had to be tended to right away. We also had to hire a septic company to inspect our system, including the leach field, to ensure that it was sound before the rebuilding could commence. In the city during a disaster, the water is generally cut off at a central location if flooding or damaged pipes are a problem.

Septic Pumping Truck

Electricity

While the electric company turned off the power to the property for safety reasons, we also had to have them come out before construction could begin so that the contractors would have power to run their equipment during the building process. Of course, a new power pole and meter had to be installed, as well as new electrical lines from the street to the future house. My husband bought a generator which the contractor used when he needed power until the electric company installed a hookup to the pole. That is the same generator that powered the well temporarily.

Natural Gas

The gas was turned off for safety reasons and during the building, the new pipes and meter were installed. When the house was finished, the gas was turned back on. We had to assure that we weren't being charged for the service while construction was being done, otherwise, we would have accrued quite a bill for the 14 months we were off the property.

Cable Television

We had to suspend our satellite television until we moved into a temporary home. The company assured us it would not be a problem to put up a new dish on the rental and they also said they would remove it when we were ready to move into our new home. The main satellite competitor charged their customers for the damaged dish so we thought our company was dealing with us fairly. However, they would not suspend our service for the duration since we were under contract, and we would have to continue our service.

Things didn't work out as they promised and they would not remove the dish from the rental after our house was finished. Thus, we had to hire somebody to remove it and repair the damage to the siding where it had been attached. We did not renew with them once our contract was up and advise you to get in writing whatever they promise. They can appear to be very sympathetic to your plight right after your loss, but how quickly they forget their promises a few months down the road!

Acquiring Tools

You will likely need a few basic tools to begin your cleanup, and those tools will depend on what kind of disaster you are dealing with. In our case, and as very often happens in other areas, the *Red Cross* and *Home Depot* were at the main crossroads with shovels, buckets, face masks, gloves, sifting boxes and rakes.

Sifting boxes, buckets, tools and water provided for the fire cleanup

They also had ice chests full of water and snacks for us to take to our property. We were so grateful to get them.

One of the items we lost which was absolutely necessary for the work we had to do on our property was a trailer to hook up behind the SUV. My husband had one made with tall sides so that it would serve for a variety of uses over the coming months. We not only hauled materials and tools to and from the site, but we also used it to move the household items we started collecting to our temporary storage unit at the urging of our adjuster.

Comfort Items

Portable Toilet

As you spend time on your devastated property, you may need a portable toilet. You will likely be spending a lot of time going through the rubble and a portable toilet will be very handy so you don't have to drive around looking for facilities.

A luxury for the workers on the burn site!

18

When you have finished your part of the cleanup, the portable toilet can be removed because the contractor will provide one for his workers as the house is built.

Sun Protection and Shelter

You may want to purchase a canopy of some kind to afford protection from the sun when you and your helpers take a break from the work. It will provide needed relief, particularly if you are hit with a summertime disaster. The canopy can also serve as protection from rain should a shower come up while you are working.

A welcome break under a canopy

Chairs and Tables

Something else you may want are a few folding chairs and a table to set your food and water on. After a fire, the ground is covered with ash, and after a flood the ground is soaking wet, so you will want some place to sit in relative comfort.

Chairs under a canopy to rest from the work

Storage Unit

If you don't have a place to store the items you will be using on your property, you may want to rent a small storage unit. Don't leave anything at the site because it could be stolen. Also, if you have a storage unit you will have a place to put items you may begin to purchase for your new home.

Shed

A shed is very useful on the property for storing tools, coolers and other items you will be using in your daily cleanup work. It provides a better option to an off-site storage unit for your tools so that you don't have to haul those items back and forth. We purchased a generator and lawn tractor right away which we had to leave on the property, so we locked them in the shed every evening before returning to the hotel.

The shed protected our supplies and tools from theft

A word to the wise about your tools

As previously mentioned, looters appear out of nowhere during situations like this, and some will take anything that isn't secured. Some of our neighbors even had their donated tools stolen. Until we got our shed, we put rakes, shovels, sifters, etc., in our car and took them with us to the hotel in the evenings rather than leave them for the looters to take. Even that didn't guarantee the tools would be safe, as some of the cars were broken into by people who knew fire victims were staying in the local hotels!

Recycling Materials

Metals

We had a dumpster delivered to our property right away for the specific purpose of collecting all the metals. Even though they were melted and no longer useful as they were, the weight added up and we got over $1000 from a recycle company for the load. This included all metals such as small appliances, pots and pans, door knobs, nails, garden tools and even small engine blocks, as well as the mangled steel barn. You might be surprised at just how much valuable metal you have, and not only does it not go to a landfill if you collect it, but you can earn a bit of cash. Our recycle company didn't charge to deliver or pick up the dumpster and they paid us for the contents.

Skid steer loading metals for recycling

Loading the barn into the dumpster for recycling

Piles of various metals for recycling

The remains of our pots and pans

We found three cast iron frying pans that had been in the family for a long time. They were pitted and in very rough shape. However, somebody suggested that we take them to a sandblaster who has a small shop in our town and that is what I did. The pans were salvaged and we happily use them often, remembering my husband's parents who used them daily before they came into our hands.

Precious Metals

Precious metals like silver and gold are a special case and need to be dealt with differently than other metals. We had sterling silver flatware and a few gold coins and other silver, as well as some jewelry which melted into a puddle during the blaze. We took the lumps of melted silver and gold to a jeweler who buys precious metals in any condition, and he assayed what we had and bought it from us at the going rate for gold and silver that day. We were surprised at the amount those few pieces brought us.

Sterling flatware found in "Fire-Proof" strongbox

Building Materials

Out of the rubble we were also able to salvage the decorative bricks that were on the front of the house. Those bricks were then used in a similar fashion on the new house.

Brother, Steve, salvaging brick

We tried to always see the positive in the events which had forever altered our lives, and one humorous thing we saw was that we now had an endless supply of firewood-- almost five acres worth. We had the trees and stumps removed from the front of the property but still had to deal with about three acres of dead trees. So the family gathered and we had a wood splitting day which resulted in enough firewood to last us several years.

Men and children worked a good part of the day to split and stack firewood

27

Getting Help

Government Agencies

When there is a large-scale disaster, County and State governments generally set up emergency response centers to serve as a clearing house for multiple levels of services and assistance. This makes good sense because it is difficult to track down each individual office (i.e.: gas, electric, phone, etc.) and these utilities generally have representatives available to handle and moderate services as needed. Also present at these centers are representatives from various non-profit agencies, insurance companies, the health department, *FEMA*, churches, the *Humane Society*, cable TV companies and others. At the El Paso County Disaster Response Center there were also donations of food, cleaning supplies, water and other items needed by those of us who were now without any possessions. We found this center to be invaluable in helping us to realize all the things we needed to tend to, many of which we wouldn't have thought of on our own, and in providing the personnel to get us started.

One thing we were advised to do was to get tetanus shots because we would be walking in the debris and wouldn't be able to see potential hazards like nails, glass, twisted metal, etc. The health department provided those shots free of charge and we opted to take them. We also acquired work boots to wear because of the hazards. You can't imagine how many nails are used in house construction until you try walking in an area that has burned. Thousands of nails are now exposed, waiting to puncture your shoes.

Churches

Valuable help came from the many churches which offered assistance. Church volunteers from various denominations came from all over the country to offer assistance in cutting trees, clearing debris and sifting ashes. These people were selfless in the gift of their compassion and hard work. They did a marvelous job. What we learned early was that you had to sign up right away for their help because with so much needing to be done and most of them having only so many days to be away from their work and families at home, a limited number of jobs would be accomplished. People who hesitated lost out, unfortunately, and were left to handle everything on their own. We were fortunate that one group came to cut down some trees, another came to help us sift ashes and yet another came to help clear debris from the barn.

Church of Christ Workers sifting through the ashes

Catholic Charities came on the scene immediately and offered help to anybody who needed it. They were ready to help to purchase items people would need straightaway, and so we asked them to purchase a shed to secure our tools and other items like our ice chest, the popup canopy, the lawn tractor and the generator. We were happy to have the peace of mind, knowing those few possessions would be less likely to be stolen. Some people who were tradesmen lost their trailers and tools, and *Catholic Charities* helped them replace some of what they needed to get back to work. *Catholic Charities* also had gift certificates to local grocery stores so that people could purchase food and supplies needed while working on their sites.

**Catholic Charities' Terri
Gray with the author**

Catholic Charities, Yazoo County, Mississippi,
Disaster Center

Southern Baptist Relief

Other Non-profit Agencies

The *Red Cross* has already been mentioned and they also opened their shelter to people without a place to go. *Goodwill Industries* had vouchers for everybody who needed them for free clothing at their stores. Considering what dirty work it was to sift ashes and move debris, this was a real help so that we would have an extra change of clothes for the next day's work. Also, since we had lost all of our clothing, we no longer had the work clothes we would normally have been able to pull out of the closet.

The *Salvation Army* had food trucks patrolling the burn area and were a welcome sight as we took a break from the grueling work before us. From their truck they dispensed sandwiches, snacks, drinks and hugs. In other areas there may be other non-profit agencies offering similar help.

Salvation Army food truck

Local food banks receive donations of food from all over the country and serve as distribution points for those needing help in this way. They often set up centers close to the affected areas so that people can get what they need. During the floods in Houston, many were located in churches.

Mental Health

It is now common practice to find mental health agencies on the scene as soon as disaster hits. There are counselors, some specializing in trauma and others in grief counseling. You will likely undergo some grief as you realize that your life has been forever altered. You will also realize that you have lost memorabilia and treasures that can never be replaced. If you have a hard time coming to grips with the experience, by all means take advantage of the help offered in this area. Experts say that after a traumatic experience one shouldn't make any major decisions for up to a year. This creates a dilemma for you because the insurance company is telling you the restoration largely has to be completed within a year. You are forced to make decisions in a time of grief. In our case, we found that starting and completing the house project was the best therapy we could have found because we were moving forward. We weren't left with much time to dwell on what had happened as we anticipated what was to come.

Animals

The *Humane Society* and other rescue agencies are often out looking for animals which have been stranded or otherwise separated from their owners. Many individuals appear from the sidelines to help take care of these animals. People with animals should contact their local *Humane Society* to find leads on where their animals might be sheltered. They can also contact rescue organizations. One thing people did as the fire was raging and they had no time to remove their large animals was to spray-paint their phone number on the side of the horses and then let them go. Many animals that escaped the blaze were reunited with their owners in the following weeks because of this.

El Paso County Sheriff's Deputy helping rescue horses from the fire

Secondary Details Checklist

- **Utilities**
  - Telephone
  - Water and Sewer
  - Electricity
  - Natural Gas
  - Cable Television
- **Acquire Tools**
- **Comfort Items**
  - Portable Toilet
  - Sun Protection and Shelter
  - Chairs and Tables
- **Storage Unit**
- **Shed**
- **Recycling Materials**
- **Precious Metals**
- **Getting Help**
  - Government Agencies
  - Churches
  - Other Non-profit Agencies
  - Mental Health
  - Animals

Flooding

*The floods have lifted up, O Lord, the floods have lifted up
their voice; the floods lift up their roaring.*
Psalm 93:3

Unless you have flood insurance, your homeowner's insurance is not likely to cover damage from flooding if the flooding results from water surges from the ocean, lake or standing water. It generally only covers water coming from above, like rain through a damaged roof.

Dealing with flooding is different than dealing with other disasters in that usually your possessions and your house are still standing, but everything is full of water and there are many hazards lurking in the mess. **Proceed with caution**. If possible, as you first enter into your home, document the damage with photographs or video. Do not take little children into the home as they are likely to handle things that may be contaminated and they would be exposed to a variety of other dangers. In some parts of the country, water snakes of different varieties could also enter the home, so if they live in your area, beware. In Houston as in other places where they exist, alligators were a concern as they sought higher shelter away from the flooded swamps.

On Your First Visit after the Flood

Do not enter your home until you have been assured by the relevant county or city authorities that it is safe to do so. A number of things have to be done to ensure your safety, such as turning off the electrical power, gas and water, and clearing out any sewage that may have come up through the drains and toilets.

- Wear mold-filtering masks because mold may have started to form in the damp environment.

- Electrical power, gas and water will likely be cut off to the property by the utility providers.

- Do not use any of your electrical appliances which will likely have been damaged by the water and may pose the risk of electrical shock if turned on. Anything electric must be thoroughly dried and cleaned and then checked out by an electrician before it can be used.

- Look for Obvious Hazards

- The ground will be saturated, so there could be dangers such as falling trees, collapsed fencing or outside walls, holes in the ground, etc.

- Depending on the extent of the flooding, the floors and walls of the house may be buckling or collapsing.

- There may be holes in the floors and items on the floor which have been carried by the flood waters inside and outside the home. Watch for sharp objects, broken glass and other debris.

Water

Any water in the house should be assumed to be contaminated by sewage and any chemicals that may have been in the house. It can make you very sick and must be evacuated as quickly as possible.

In the event you have a well, do not drink the water until it has been inspected. Sewage and other hazards may have seeped in through the well head and it must be checked out before you can use it.

Your local county or city authorities may establish procedures for dealing with the items that must be discarded. Please follow their directives for the safety and wellbeing of yourself and others.

Documents

Many experts advise you to place any valuable papers that have been wet into short stacks between cardboard and then placing them in a freezer. If left long enough, they should dry pretty well, though they won't ever look like they did before the flood. Of course, you won't be able to use your own freezer until it as well as the house has been checked out, so you may want to ask a friend to keep these items for you. Papers that have been contaminated with sewage should not be put in the freezer. It is best to try to air dry these and then replace them, being careful to wear rubber gloves when handling them.

Photographs

It is likely that you will not have time to immediately deal with lots of photographs, but you will want to at least try to salvage some of them. Rinse them off in clean water, and then place them between layers of wax paper in a stack, and then put them in a Ziploc bag. They can then be put in the freezer to save for the time you can return to work with them. When that time comes, it is recommended that you lay them on paper towels on a table inside the house away from sun and other elements, and let them dry. If you don't freeze them, they are likely to mold.

Cleaning Up

If you have flood insurance, the company should take care of the cleanup of your property. They will have a water damage restoration company go into your home and evacuate all the water. This will not only rid the house of the standing water, but they will bring in wet/dry vacuums and dehumidifier machines to dry out the rugs and furniture, as well as fans to dry the walls, ceilings, floors, etc. Depending on the amount of water, this process can take days to weeks to accomplish. Particularly if the ground is saturated, the process will take longer as there will be continued seepage into the foundation.

If you are doing your own cleanup, you will need gloves and masks, cleaning supplies of all kinds like mops, squeegees, buckets, plastic garbage bags, disinfectants and large tubs for disinfecting your linens, clothing and other cloth items. You will need a place to hang these items once they have been washed and disinfected as well.

You may need to rent dehumidifiers, a sump pump, fans, heaters and other equipment for drying out your furnishings and house. Follow all instructions carefully so that you do the best job possible and salvage as much as you can. Remember not to use any electrical appliance that was in the house before the flood as it could be damaged and cause you great harm. Do not use your furnace until it has been inspected, and keep the temperature in the house cool until you have removed all the water to delay the growth of mold. You will want to keep the house well ventilated until it is completely dried out. Below are basic things to do after the flood waters have subsided. Please consult Appendix 2 for sources for detailed instructions and advice on how to proceed to ensure that your home will be habitable before you move back in.

Removing Debris

- Many items will be damaged beyond repair. Carefully bag them up for removal. You will likely have to remove the drywall and insulation behind it for replacement. If you don't remove these, you will develop problems with mold which will require even more extensive repairs later on. It is recommended that you cut between 6 and 20 inches above the top water line. For further instructions please refer to my resource guide.

- Rinse dirt and mud off all items that won't be further damaged by the addition of more water.

- Using detergent and water in a bucket with a bit of disinfectant, wipe down all hard surfaces and walls and then be sure to rinse them with clean water.

- You may have a floor drain in your utility or laundry room which will need to be flushed out and disinfected. It may be clogged with debris, but you may be able to use the wet/dry vacuum to suck out the debris and then flush it with either a hose or a bucket of water. Be sure to disinfect the drain.

Cleaning up after flooding in Missouri

Rugs, Carpets and Upholstered Furniture

- Remove all rugs and dry as quickly as possible. If sewage is involved, they will have to be washed and disinfected. They may have to be discarded.

- Carpets and pads will have to be removed if sewage is involved. Otherwise, a professional carpet cleaner may be able to salvage the carpet, but he will likely have to replace the pad.

- You will have to hire a professional to see if your larger upholstered furniture can be salvaged. If possible, in the meantime, put such furniture up on blocks and direct the fans toward them to accelerate drying.

- Mattresses, pillows, etc. and most upholstered items should be discarded if they have come in contact with flood waters. Even if the upholstery could be saved, the foam or other padding inside the furniture will be contaminated.

Furnishings removed from flooded house in Minnesota

Other Furniture

- If your furniture is made with pressed board, it cannot be salvaged once it has warped from water. It will have to be discarded.
- Wooden furniture may survive if you get it cleaned up and dried. As with your cupboards and closets,

open up any dressers, cabinets or drawers so that they can dry gradually. You don't want to put them out in the sun where they might dry too quickly and split. You may have to refinish some of the surfaces, depending on how they were originally finished.

Mold

One of the major concerns in a home after flooding is the growth of mold which can lead to illness. Therefore it must be dealt with from the start.

- Always wear gloves and a spore-filtering face mask when you are dealing with mold.

- If you have the space, you can freeze valuable documents and books to prevent the growth of mold until you have the time to deal with them.

- Mold spores can be killed with rubbing alcohol.

**Mold damage on ceiling
after Hurricane Katrina**

Food and medicine

- Any foods that are not in commercially sealed cans must be discarded because the polluted water poses an extreme risk to health.

- Undamaged canned foods can be kept but the cans must be washed and disinfected before using.

- All medicines and toiletries that have been exposed to water must be disposed of.

Before Moving Back In

Removal of the debris and drying up of the water are only the beginning of your recovery. Please don't try to move back into your home until you have been assured of the following:

- The regular water supply has been inspected and declared safe for use by the authorities.

- A thorough electrical inspection of the house has been done. Remember, all the wiring in the house may have been wet by the waters and no outlets should be used till they are checked out. Consult your power company for instructions on how to accomplish this.

- Every room has been dried, decontaminated and cleaned, including walls, counters, cabinets, fixtures, and floors.

- All household **contents**, including but not limited to dishes, pots, linens, clothing, tools, toys, tricycles, bicycles, etc. have been thoroughly washed and disinfected - either by using boiling water or by using a sterilizing solution of one part chlorine bleach to four parts water. Rinse everything thoroughly.

- The plumbing has been inspected and certified for use.

Flood evacuation by boat in Missouri

Flooding Checklist

- [ ] **Water**
- [ ] **Documents**
- [ ] **Photographs**
- [ ] **Cleaning up**
  - o Removing Debris
  - o Rugs, Carpets and Upholstered Furniture
  - o Other Furniture
  - o Mold
  - o Food and Medicine

After a Hurricane or Tornado

*Then they cried to the LORD in their trouble, and
he delivered them from their distress. He made
the storm be still, and the waves of the sea were
hushed.*
Psalm 107:28-29

Hurricanes and tornadoes present their own set of insurance problems because of the different kinds of damage they do to property. The high winds often dismantle roofs and siding, and they take down trees, power lines and other structures. In some cases they completely destroy the home. If the insurance policy has a **rider** for wind damage, those things are likely to be covered. But then comes the water. Water falling through a roof might be covered by insurance, but as often happens, water coming from rising waters and ocean surges and other bodies of water is not covered. Flooding damage is not covered unless the homeowner carries flood insurance, most of which is purchased from the United States government.

The same rules apply when entering a home after a hurricane or tornado that apply after a flood. Please refer to that section if there is anything left of your home to salvage.

In the event of a hurricane, one thing that sometimes happens is that in a multi-story house, the lowest level will be damaged by flood waters while the upper story remains

47

intact. The whole structure may have sustained wind damage which can be repaired. If the house is going to be salvaged, all the flood-damaged contents must be removed. If the work is going to be done by a contractor and the house is not habitable, the contractor may require that all the contents of the house be removed because he won't want to be liable for any theft or damage to the contents. Every piece of upholstered furniture, every mattress, every pillow and anything that holds water will be very heavy and difficult to move.

After a hurricane or tornado hits, many people will be scrambling to find help of all kinds. Contractors and supplies will be in short supply. Even storage units might be filled up quickly. It is very important to start your recovery quickly, as soon as you are cleared by local authorities to go in to your property. There will be many people in the same situation and there are only so many resources available.

Because flooding often accompanies tornadoes and hurricanes, please refer to the _Flooding Checklist_ for the things you need to do.

**Tornado damaged house in
Louisiana**
48

Smoke Damage

I think there will be more smiles when the smoke clears.
Shaun Alexander

Sometimes a fire doesn't consume a house and its contents, but it causes smoke damage. This type of damage can be difficult to deal with. There may be soot and ash as well as the strong odor of smoke. The soot and ash may be oily, or it may have gotten wet from fire suppressant chemicals or water. It may permeate upholstery, mattresses, carpets and drapery as well as other porous materials. Cleaning it up is not just a matter of vacuuming the walls and washing them down.

Damage to the structure of the house like the roof or drywall will be covered under the dwelling portion of your home owner's policy. Damage to the contents of your house will be covered under the contents portion of the policy.

Often the ash and soot as well as the smoke odor can be removed by a commercial cleaning service, and that is the likely route the insurance company will try first. However, if you are not satisfied with the results of commercial cleaning, insist that the items which still retain the odor of smoke are replaced. Be sure to check the limits of your homeowner's policy to see just what your policy covers. If you have allergies or asthma or other health concerns, be sure to have the home inspected by a qualified individual to ensure that the offending substances have truly been removed.

Smoke Damage Checklist

Not only the soot and ash, but all odors from the smoke must be removed. If you are not satisfied, insist that the items be replaced.

- ☐ **Carpets**
- ☐ **Curtains**
- ☐ **Furniture**
- ☐ **Drywall**

Insurance Details

*Insurance is the only product that both the buyer and seller
hope is never actually used.*
Unknown

Insurance companies vary greatly in their response to
the plight of their customers, so you might encounter
anything from a quick helpful response to a wait-and-see
attitude from a less than enthusiastic adjuster.   We
personally experienced and heard stories of both kinds and
everything in between, so be prepared to advocate for
yourself in the event you get the "wait-and-see" type. If
you don't think your adjuster is working on your behalf,
or if he doesn't offer the kind of help you need in sorting
through your claim, ask the company to assign you a
different person. They will generally do that without
hesitation.

Coverage for Property

You must know what kind of **coverage** you have.
Your homeowner's policy will spell out exactly what is
covered, and you will need all the help you can get, so
review it with your adjuster thoroughly. Be sure to read
the section on **exclusions**. Particularly where water
damage is concerned, it can be very confusing as to what
is covered. For instance, some policies exclude damage
caused by "wind-driven" water (i.e.: hurricanes). Some
exclude water damage caused by water coming up through
sewers and drains. Some policies don't cover any flooding
unless you have specific flood coverage. Some exclude

damage caused by moving earth (i.e.: landslides and earthquakes).

Replacement Cost or Fair Market Value?

The other thing you will need to determine is whether your policy covers replacement cost or fair **market value**. (See Appendix 1) **Replacement cost coverage** is more expensive, but it usually covers your rebuild for a comparable house and your contents for similar contents. The fair market value depreciates what you had and won't cover your rebuild completely. It will also depreciate your contents, and most items over 10 years old are devalued by about 90%. The 10% you get is what your contents would sell for on the open market at any given time. This becomes very important when you get down to the nitty-gritty of filing your claim. (See the section on Content Listing).

If you decide to move into a different house or build elsewhere, be aware that you will lose the value of your land. In other words, you may get the cost to rebuild your house, but you can't take the land with you, and whatever value it has will be deducted from your payout. We were told that could account for up to 20% of the value of our property.

If you have replacement cost coverage, the items must actually be replaced in order to receive the full replacement cost. For example, if an $800 sound system is destroyed, the insurance company will pay the **actual cash value** amount, say $600, until the sound system is replaced. When it is replaced and the receipt is produced, the insurance company will pay the difference up to the replacement amount. This, of course, is subject to any limitations listed in the replacement coverage section of your insurance policy. If your insurance covers fair-market value, you may only get $500 or less for the same system, taking into account the depreciation of the item.

Out-buildings

If you had outbuildings, a detached gazebo or playground equipment, you will want to see if they were covered. You may have had a greenhouse, shed or a barn or separate shop. Be sure to ascertain exactly what your coverage for those was as well. Then, based on your policy, you will have to decide whether or not to replace them.

Coverage for Loss of Use

If **loss of use** is covered, temporary housing will be provided. Your insurance company may leave it up to you to find that housing. On the other hand, they may find it for you. Either way, you must get on this as soon as possible, because every other victim of the same catastrophe will be looking for housing as well. In the situation we were in, some people had to accept temporary housing quite a distance away from their work and property because the rentals and hotels close by were immediately snatched up. The housing provided should be more or less comparable in size and amenities to the house you lost if available.

Coverage for Miscellaneous Expenses

Some insurance will cover your expenses for things like food and laundry while you are in a hotel waiting to move into a rental house or apartment. If that is the case, you need to be sure to document your expenses carefully because you won't be paid for anything you can't justify. Some items, like clothing for instance, will not be covered as an expense but will be covered under your "contents" payout. You will want to be very careful not to overspend on immediate needs, because the contents portion of your payout will quickly diminish.

Coverage for Livestock

Unless you carry livestock insurance which covers loss of animals due to fire or other natural disasters, you will generally not be reimbursed for any animals which die or are lost in such an event. Homeowners' policies do not cover livestock or other animals, so if you have them, you should definitely buy coverage under a separate policy.

Special Riders

You may have had special riders for items like fine art, jewelry, musical instruments, firearms, antique clocks, furs, and other items of higher value which have stricter limits under the regular homeowner's policy. Contact the insurer of those items if it is different than the insurance company managing your homeowner's policy.

Rebekah with the remains of our grand piano

Automobiles and other Vehicles

Your car and other vehicles (if you had them) will have been covered under a different policy and will not be covered under a homeowner's policy unless you had a special rider for them. This will also include motorcycles, camping trailers and motor homes. If you had a small trailer for hauling lumber, garden supplies, and the like, that will probably be covered by your homeowners policy. Larger trailers for hauling automobiles, livestock, etc., would be covered with special trailer insurance.

Vehicles going through flood waters in Houston

Receipts

From the first moment you are out of your home till your claim is settled, you must save all your receipts. This can be a nightmare for you so it is a good idea to quickly set up a filing system for all of them. It can be as simple as a filing box with dividers labeled "food," "laundry," "transportation," "housing," "contents," etc. You may be asked to provide all these receipts to the insurance company on a weekly, monthly or one-time basis, so it is imperative that they be available. You will quickly find yourself with hundreds of pieces of paper which must be managed in some way. You can paper-clip them together by the week so that if you have to find a specific receipt, you will at least be able to narrow down the location.

We discovered a wonderful product called a NEAT scanner which extracts the date, source and totals from the receipts as they are scanned and allows you to create files for each category. With the capability of creating reports it was an invaluable tool in keeping our records straight and at the end, we were able to submit not only a detailed report of all our expenses by category, but also digital copies of the receipts to back up our claims. Our adjuster said he wished everybody would do something similar because it is not efficient to have to sort through a manila envelope full of various types of receipts. We have continued to use the NEAT scanner for our home bookkeeping and use the same process for filing our income tax every year. While the scanner is no longer available from NEAT, they have a subscription program which accomplishes the same thing online using your own scanner or smart phone. Looking back, we can hardly imagine how we could have managed without one. It was an expense that saved us hours of time and kept us organized. There are apps you can get which also do a similar job of helping you organize receipts, using your phone. Please see Appendix 2 for more information.

Managing Insurance Payouts Carefully

One of the advantages of submitting an expense report to your insurance company on a semi-monthly or monthly basis is that you will be reimbursed as you go along. Expenses quickly add up if you are paying for everything out of pocket. Sometimes the checks will be large and the temptation is to spend all the money on impulse buying. Please don't fall into that trap because there is a limit to what the insurance will pay. It is a good idea to put the checks into the bank and handle your spending carefully.

Maximizing Insurance Payouts

In the section, *Contents,* I explain the most complex part of working with insurance because you will want to ensure that you get every penny your policy allows. If you have a mortgage on your house, the insurance money for the rebuild will go to the mortgage lender, credit union or bank, and they will disperse the construction funds as needed. That first check that you are issued right after the disaster has to be turned over to the mortgage lender, because it actually belongs to them, unless of course, you don't have a mortgage. If you don't want your mortgage to increase you will need to build within your means. The temptation to build "bigger and better" is very attractive, but you will increase your debt load greatly if you aren't careful. It is amazing how difficult it is to stay within the limits of your allowance when all the latest innovations and materials are offered to you. If you want some of those things you will either have to cut somewhere else or deal with a larger mortgage to pay for them.

Not only will you receive (in most cases) the initial payment to begin your rebuild, but you will also receive a partial payment for the contents you lost. Since the rebuild money will go to the mortgage company, the other check will be what you will use to start rebuilding your wardrobe and basic possessions. Move slowly and budget carefully. You will discover just how valuable your household goods and clothing were when you begin the arduous task of replacing them, and the money will be used up quickly.

Insurance Details Checklist

☐ **Coverage for Property**
☐ **Replacement Cost or Fair Market Value?**
☐ **Out-buildings**
☐ **Coverage for Loss of Use**
☐ **Coverage for Miscellaneous Expenses**
☐ **Coverage for Livestock**
☐ **Special Riders**
☐ **Automobiles and other Vehicles**
☐ **Receipts**

Contents

The things you own end up owning you. It's only after you
lose everything that you're free to do anything.
Chuck Palahniuk

We learned that the standard for many insurance policies was that the value of the contents of the house was roughly half the value of the house itself. So for instance, if the house was valued at $400,000, the contents were valued at $200,000 and that would be the figure you would have to work with in reclaiming your money. You might have been given half of that, or $100,000, and told to start accumulating your furnishings because the process needed to be tied up in a year. In order to recover the remaining half, or $100,000, you would need to list your losses on a spreadsheet with specific information to justify your claim.

Replace and Forget

One way to avoid the tedious listing process is to just submit receipts for a few of the most valuable items you replaced and forget the rest. You might collect quite a bit that way or only a small fraction of what you could get if you do a complete list. The choice is yours.

List and Collect

Before we knew that our insurance company would provide a consultant to come to our home and walk us

60

through the listing process, we started listing our household goods using a generic form we found on the internet. After we had spent several weeks creating our list, our adjuster asked if we would like to have help. Of course we said yes, and he arranged for a consultant to come give us a few pointers on how to complete this tedious process. We were very grateful for the help we got and it made the process a little less daunting. One of the first things this gentleman asked me was what was in our bedroom. I said, "A bed, two tables, two lamps, a chair, etc." Then, he said:

> *"You have to think in a different way when you are listing. What was on your bed? What kind of bedding did you have, etc.? You had a wood headboard and footboard, a bed frame, a box spring, a mattress, a mattress cover, a bottom sheet, a top sheet, a blanket, a bedspread, two pillows, two pillow cases, etc."*

I was stunned, but he was right. We would have to replace every single item, not just a generic bed. So all those items went onto the list. Unfortunately, we had already submitted a partial list before we got the help, so some of the items we were initially paid for were undervalued. Most of the people we spoke with got little or no guidance and had to muddle through as best they could with their listing, so we felt blessed to have this bonus from our insurance company.

Learn to Use a Spreadsheet

The idea of listing household belongings seems unreasonable and somehow unfair since you have been paying monthly premiums to insure what you had. That doesn't matter—the insurance companies seek to manage their losses and so they put the burden on your shoulders to justify your claim. If you don't "do it their way" they win and you lose. It is pretty simple. So you play by their rules and begin with a blank spreadsheet. The formats may differ slightly from one company to the next, but they are similar to the one shown on page 66. Some companies may even send you their format by email so you won't have to make adjustments later. In the first column you list the room the item was in. Next you name or describe the item, using the brand if known. In the third column you list the value or price paid for the item. In the fourth column you list the age. In succeeding columns you list the source, quantity, replacement cost, condition and so forth. You won't have all the information on every item, so just leave those spaces blank. However, the more information you have, the easier it will be to process your claim. We were told that these lists are actually sent to offshore locations where labor is cheap and they check out the values of the items listed. By listing the vendor with a hyperlink, it makes it much easier to confirm the value of your items. Sometimes we had to list *eBay* as a source because most of our furniture items were no longer available in stores due to their age.

Correct Descriptions Matter

The first item on the list on the following page was a Baldwin Spinet Piano which had been in the family for about 60 years. We found one online selling for $900 so that is the replacement cost we listed. The insurance company disagreed with the value, saying it was only worth $300. Then, because it was over 10 years old, they depreciated it by 90%, leaving us with a payment of $30. The mistake we made with that item was in the description. If we had described it "**vintage**" as it was, we would have gotten replacement value!

	A	B	C	D	E	F	G
1	Description	brand	Vendor	quantity	Age year	Age Month	Insured piece per item
2	Baldwin Acrosonic piano Spinet Light Brown SatinApprox Size36 inches tall Piano	Baldwin	Baldwin	1	60		$ 900.00
	Gustav Becker Vienna regulator. Gustav Becker 8 day weight						

Sample listing sheet

There are many online resources for determining the value of your lost items. I found this one for the above mentioned piano as I was researching for this book.

Baldwin Acrosonic Appraisal Listings

This is the only used piano guide on the internet as to what a piano is worth. It is used extensively as the source of used piano price information by retailers, piano appraisers, piano teachers, and piano technicians. It is a fast, free, and convenient way to look up the average price of a used piano. This is an example of the appraisal service by the Bluebook of Pianos.

The prices are stated in U.S. Dollars and are based on market values based on comparisons of used pianos, and offered for sale on the internet on such sites as Craig's List, E Bay or in classified ads in newspapers throughout the United States and Canada. These pianos are also advertised on the web by technicians, private parties, music stores teachers, and on auctions or liquidations.

The Acrosonic piano is the largest selling piano brand name and model of all time. This distinctive and exclusive name designates a line of spinet and console pianos built by the Baldwin Piano Company. Coined from the Greek word,"akros," meaning supreme and the Latin word, "sonus," meaning tone, the trade mark "Acrosonic" is registered in the United States Patent Office.

Baldwin Acrosonic Supreme Tone Spinet Piano, 36 inches tall, bearing serial number 527747, manufactured in 1953. Well cared for and in good condition. When this piano is tuned for maximum performance the value is $1,550.00. Figure is based on the age, condition, size, grade and rarity of this piano.

http://www.bluebookofpianos.com/acrosonic-sampler.html

We discovered that there were a couple of ways to go about listing in order to receive the maximum amount allowed by your policy. It is likely that you won't replace every item, but you need the total value of your claim to exceed the policy value to ensure that you will get the full amount. When you see the depreciation of your **personal property**, you will feel very let down and you will understand why you may have to put so much effort into this process.

The following page shows a sample of the listing required by our insurance company. You can see that it is very detailed. We added a column with the internet links to similar items in order to facilitate substantiation of our claim. Because of the number of columns, it was not possible to show the entire entry on one line in this format. The bottom example picks up on column L from the top example.

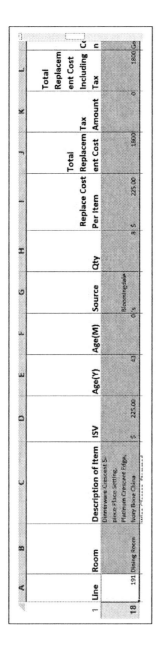

	A	B	C	D	E	F	G	H	I	J	K	L
	Line	Room	Description of Item	ISV	Age(Y)	Age(M)	Source	Qty	Replace Cost Per Item	Total Replacem ent Cost	Tax Amount	Total Replacem ent Cost Including Tax
18	191	Dining Room	Dinnerware Crescent 5-piece Place Setting, Platinum Crescent Edge, Ivory Bone China Italia Classe Charm...	$ 225.00	43		Bloomingdale 0's	8	$ 225.00	1800	0	1800 Go

	L	M	N	O	P	Q	R	S	T	U	V
1	Total Replacem ent Cost Including Tax	Conditio n	Total Depreciation %	Total Depreciat ion Amount Including Tax	Actual Cash Value Including Tax (ACV)	ACV after Item Limit Including Tax	Receipt Amount	Over/Unde r		Recoverable Payout	Adjusted Replacement cost
18	1800/Good		0.9	1.00	$ 180.00	$ 180.00	190.00	$ (1,800.00)	$ 0	$ (1,800.00) $	(190.00) $

66

The previous pictures illustrate a spread sheet with the entry for the china which was devalued 90%

Line 18 on the list on page 66 shows the replacement cost of eight 5-piece place settings of fine china which were part of the set of china we got when married 43 years before. The china is valuable and still available. Each place setting costs $225 to replace as verified by the website. Since there were eight, the total value was $1800. However, because of the age of the china, it was depreciated 90%. That gave us a whopping $180 for the actual cash value, and that is the amount paid to us for the china. We had not had it 50 years or more and it wasn't really unique, so it couldn't be considered vintage.

At the outset we had been advised to list our contents room by room, starting at the doorway and walking our eyes to the right around every item in the room, into every closet and drawer from top to bottom. That is what we did and how we initially listed what we had. It was very tedious to recall what was in the "lower, left-hand drawer of the desk" and on and on. Think about it for a moment. A typical desk will have at least one drawer with pens and pencils in it. Do you know how many? It might have a drawer with miscellaneous office supplies such as paper clips, a ruler, a stapler, staples, etc. Do you know how many? It might also have a drawer with computer paper in it. Do you know how much? On the top of the desk there may have been a computer. Do you remember the brand, age and value? How about the external hard drive? Did you actually keep it there rather than securing it away from the computer? Personal experience is speaking here.

Our external hard drive burned alongside the computer it was backing up!

Think about a drawer in your dresser. Do you know how many pairs of socks, underwear, t-shirts, etc. are in it? And by the way, could you please try to remember the brand names? When you make your list, you will be asked these questions. We had to list everything because our total depreciated amount had to equal or exceed the amount allowed by our policy.

A Better Strategy

After the consultant came we learned a different strategy. He said to begin the listing with the most valuable items in the house. Were there any **antiques**? He said to list those first because antiques don't depreciate! There might have been a very expensive bedroom set in the house, but if it was over 10 years old but not antique or vintage, it would depreciate 90% and be virtually worthless, while Grandma's 110-year-old-dresser would earn its total value. So list all antiques first, and remember, **antiques must be 100 years or older.**

The next thing he told us was to list all "vintage" items. Vintage items must have some artistic or collectible worth. So, for instance, while that Baldwin piano was only worth $30 in the end, the ALF stuffed toy that our son once had brought $90! A small ceramic pitcher in the shape of an elephant made in 1949 was worth $60 as verified by a similar one on *eBay*.

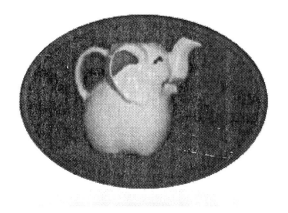

1949 ceramic elephant pitcher

**Stuffed Alf animal that was worth 3 times
what a 1950s Baldwin piano was valued**

The reason it is good to do the listing this way is that if you take care of all the more valuable items first, you may not be compelled to list absolutely everything in order to bring your total up to or past the amount allowed by your policy. If your policy allows up to $200,000 and you have already listed $220,000, you don't need to continue. Our advisor told us it was best to list beyond the allowed amount by at least 10% just in case some items were depreciated more than we anticipated.

If you find yourself in a position to have to list the minutiae, there are things you can do to help yourself along. Our daughter suggested we go to a local bed and bath store and establish a "wedding registry." By doing that we accomplished two things at once. Using the barcode scanner they gave us, we scanned all the items we remembered having in the kitchen and bath. That information helped us to create the list of lost items along with the relevant information we needed for the insurance company. It also provided a list for the many people who asked what we needed to restock our home. We could send them to the store to look up our registry and it made it easy for them to shop. Of course, as we transferred the information to our inventory list, we also had to list the approximate ages and conditions of the items we lost.

If you had a lot of tools in a workshop or garage, you could go to a home-improvement store and create a similar list. Walking up and down the aisles would help jog your memory as to what you had before it was all lost.

After our list was submitted and verified by the insurance company, it was sent back to us with their assessment of the value of our contents. We had the opportunity to go through it and appeal if their values didn't agree with ours. Once the total reached our maximum, those details didn't matter and we got the full payout.

V	W	X
isted acement cost	Link	Comment
-		We object to the 90% depreciation set by AmFam. This set of china was rarely used over the course of our marriage and was in as good a condition as new.
92.50		Please add $20.50 shipping to the price.

Our unsuccessful objection to the devaluation of our china

In Appendix 2, under "Sample Forms for Processing Claims," you will find a link to United Policy Holders. They have a spreadsheet which you can download to begin your list. The lists are pretty standard from one insurance company to the other, and if your insurance company doesn't require a specific list, this spreadsheet will suffice.

The Payoff

Was all the effort worth it? Absolutely it was. We needed to recover all our contents money so that we could furnish the house. But we also had some hard decisions to make about what would be replaced because at today's prices, there wasn't enough money to replace everything. Also, we had time to re-evaluate our priorities during those months that the house was being rebuilt, and we decided that we had entirely too much stuff. Since our children were no longer at home, we decided that the bedrooms would each be furnished with a bed, a chair and a dresser to be available for guests, but there would be nothing in the dresser drawers or closets. We no longer needed as many linens, dishes or craft items, so we didn't replace all of those things which had occupied those drawers and closets.

Using Content Money

Before we understood how the system works, we thought we had to replace every item we had in order to be reimbursed. We didn't understand that the important thing was for us to get the maximum content money allowed by our policy. So initially we made a few mistakes by buying things like small appliances which were practically identical to what we had. We thought if we had the receipts we would break even. However, we learned that we should have tried to get everything we could at the best price possible, because after we reached the maximum allowed, that would be it, no matter what we spent. If we had not listed, then those receipts would have backed up our purchases and we would have been paid on a per item basis. But it was definitely better for us to do the listing and we received the maximum allowed.

Our house cost more to build than we received in settlement, so we had to come up with some money to cover the increased cost without going into further debt. Since our listing of contents resulted in more than 10% above our allowance, we got the full amount allowed by the policy and decided to use part of that to pay for the extras on the house rather than on more contents. We had made a decision not to replace everything we had lost and we saw this as an opportunity to simplify, so we used about 20% of the content money on the construction of the house.

How that money is spent is an individual decision. Some people choose to upgrade some of the contents and cut back on others. We had to use some of the content money to cover the cost of dead tree removal, chipping and the grinding of remaining stumps. Some people cut back on everything and use the content money for other things like travel. The important thing to remember is that once the money is spent, it is gone and the insurance company will not give you any more.

Contents Checklist

- ☐ **Replace and Forget**
- ☐ **List and Collect**
- ☐ **Learn to Use a Spreadsheet**
- ☐ **Use Correct Descriptions**
- ☐ **List Antiques**
- ☐ **List Vintage Items**

Replacing Household Goods

*By knowledge the rooms are filled with all
precious and pleasant riches.*
Proverbs 24:4

You may choose to buy everything new and use a source like *Amazon* or other online retailers. This works well for many items and if you are a Prime member, you won't pay for shipping.

Local Retailers

You may decide to purchase your furniture and other household items locally, or if you aren't in a city, at the closest city to where you live. That is a good option and gives you the opportunity to negotiate with local merchants, particularly if you are buying a houseful of furnishings. It also gives you the opportunity to see exactly what you will be getting. It was our experience that many local shops offered discounts for a limited amount of time to people who had lost their homes during the fire.

Donations from Local Relief Groups

In our area, several organizations collected household furnishings to give to people who had lost their homes. They had furniture, kitchen utensils, pots and pans, small appliances and dishes. What they had was free for the taking and helped many people who didn't have the resources or insurance to cover what they needed.

Estate Sales

We chose to purchase the bulk of our furniture from estate sales because we could find items that were similar to what we had before the fire. We even found nice dishes and flatware, as well as garden tools and some small appliances which were in excellent condition. We also found clothing, some of with the tags on. Estate sales are a great resource and in some areas are known as tag sales. To find them in your area, go to estatesales.net and select your state and city. You will be amazed at the wonderful things you can find at very reasonable prices.

First piece of furniture purchased after the fire

Thrift Stores

Thrift Stores are another good source for home furnishings and clothing. They exist in practically every city and town across America now. The larger ones are *Goodwill Industries, Disabled American Vets* and *Arc Thrift Stores.*

Newspapers or Online Sellers

Some areas have print papers where every kind of merchandise is sold. In our area we have the *Thrifty Nickel.* These little papers can usually be found in grocery stores and gas stations and they are free. Another source which many people have found invaluable is *Craigslist.* You can google *Craigslist* with the name of your city and you should be able to search for whatever you want. Sellers usually include pictures with their "for sale" listing, and often people are willing to negotiate their prices.

Replacing Household Goods Checklist

   ☐ **Local Retailers**
   ☐ **Donations**
   ☐ **Estate Sales**
   ☐ **Thrift Stores**
   ☐ **Newspapers or Online Sellers**

Rebuilding

For every house is built by someone,
but the builder of all things is God.
Hebrews 3:4

If you have decided to rebuild rather than move to a different location, you will need to decide how to proceed. Again, you are being forced to make decisions while you are still coming to grips with what has happened, and you may still be grieving. So what are some of the reasons for moving ahead quickly?

- The insurance company might require you to be finished within a year.

- The demand is immediate and the supply can't always meet the demand for contractors, architects and materials.

- If you put it off, you may use up your insurance money and have nothing left at the end. You won't get the second half of the value of your policy if you don't rebuild.

- You will prolong your grief and find yourself in a worse position at the end of the year than you were right after the disaster hit.

It is never easy to make decisions during a crisis, and some decisions may have to be postponed. But the reality is that the insurance companies expect you to move on, and the penalties for not doing so can be severe. If you had a $400,000 rebuild policy and you don't follow through, you may just end up with the half that your adjuster gave you in the beginning and forfeit the rest. You can't rebuild a comparable home with half the money. It may seem heartless, but if there were no "encouragement" to move forward from the insurance company, the claims process could drag out for years, and they won't allow that to happen. Another thing to consider is that seeing progress in your recovery is a form of healing therapy in itself. If you take control of what you can, you will feel much better about the situation knowing a new home will be yours within a few months.

Demolition

Before we could start rebuilding, all the debris had to be removed. We combed the property for all metals which could be recycled as detailed under the section "Secondary Details." However, there was still a lot to be cleaned up— all the items that weren't metal like the porcelain fixtures, the remains of dishes, the fireplace, the ash and of course, the foundation. We hired a demolition company and were grateful we had the **additional coverage** in our policy to cover the cost of demolition and debris removal. This is one of those items you may not think about when buying homeowner's insurance, but in the event you need it, it is worth a lot more than the cost of the premiums.

After our first view of the devastation, this was the hardest thing for me to watch

Tract Builder

You may select a builder who does tract homes. Those companies generally have a few stock house plans from which you can choose. Within certain prescribed limits they will allow you to make decisions about colors, fixtures, cosmetic features, flooring, tiling and kitchen counters, cabinets and appliances. Occasionally they will allow you to change the configuration of a few walls or other construction details, but you pretty much have to choose your plan and go with it. This is a good option if money is tight and you don't have time to spend on the job site.

Self-Contract

You may decide to contract the house yourself. Unless you have some experience in this area, this could be very risky. One of the problems is that building sub-contractors like framers, electricians, plumbers, etc., will have more work than they can handle after a widespread disaster, and they often look to general contractors to line up their jobs. When work is abundant, it is difficult to find somebody willing to do an isolated job. It is tricky to schedule subcontractors efficiently so that construction proceeds at an orderly rate and without conflicting schedules. This is not to say it is impossible, but it requires a lot of skill and patience.

Online House Plans

You can find house plans online for a cost, and that is an option if you don't want to hire an architect. In Appendix 2 you will find a couple of websites with ideas of what is available. You can key in the features you want and the sites will bring up many options of styles and prices for you to consider. If you like the house you lost but don't have the architectural plans, you might be able to recover them from your local County or City Building Office. Our house was too old for that, so we had to start over.

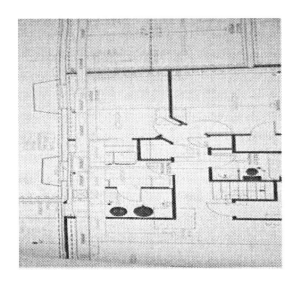

Building plans show interior floor plans and exterior elevations

Getting the house plans is just the beginning of your building process. Those plans have to be approved by your local County or City Building Office. You will be charged a fee for that process and after any discrepancies are noted and/or corrected, the plans will be stamped "approved." At that time, for a fee, you will be issued a building permit which will have to be visible and available through every step of the construction. Inspectors from the various trades (concrete, framing, electrical, plumbing) will be going to your building site to ensure that the foundation, utilities, plumbing, electrical, framing, etc., are all being done to code. As they pass each phase, the inspector will sign off on the permit. The building permit will have an expiration date, and if you go over that, you will have to apply for an extension.

Choosing a Contractor/Builder

However you decide to design your house, once you have your plans drawn up, it is time to begin to interview contractors. You should collect recommendations from people you know, check out any potential contractors through the *Better Business Bureau*, visit homes they have built and read reviews. One of the benefits of the internet is that you can usually find a lot of information and critiques of contractors and developers which you can sift through.

Beware of contractors who are not established in your area. There are many horror stories about people who have hired "fly-by-night" roofers, framers and other contractors who arrive on the scene right after a disaster and disappear just as quickly, leaving you with no recourse in case there are problems.

The Interview

You have decided on your house design, you know what you are going to get from the insurance company, and now it is time to choose the builder. How do you proceed?

Please see Appendix 5 for a list of questions to ask potential contractors. During the interview, be aware of how you and he relate to each other. Sometimes there are personality clashes. Sometimes you have a gut feeling that you wouldn't be able to work together or that he wouldn't listen to you down the road. This is your house, and he is to work for you, not the other way around. Pay attention to those instincts. You don't want to start construction and then find out that your builder wants you to stay away until the house is finished. You may discover as time goes on that there are slight changes you would like to make. In order for this to happen, you need to have a good rapport with him and the freedom to consult with him throughout the process. You should be able to talk to the builder and see what is possible. Sometimes he will charge a fee to make the changes and you have to decide if you want to pay the fee or forego the changes. Once you have signed a contract and the building has commenced, it is very difficult to turn back or get a new builder without a possible legal battle.

A word to the wise

   You want to get bids for building the house you want. Do not tell the contractor up front how much money you will have for the project! You want an estimate based on the amount he says he needs to accomplish the job. If you give him a dollar amount, he will likely build to that amount, and it could possibly end up costing more. There always seem to be hidden costs and you want to have a bit of flexibility in the decisions you will be making as the building progresses.

You will not get a bid on the same day you do the interview, but you should expect to receive detailed bids on the cost to rebuild within a week or two. Your bids will show not only the total cost to rebuild but should be complete with specific allowances for things like the contractor's fee, the foundation, the framing, the roof, electric fixtures, plumbing fixtures, flooring, painting, counters, appliances, cabinets, grading the land after construction, etc. You will want to compare the bids carefully. Price isn't always the main reason for choosing one over the other. Additional factors like reputation, availability and rapport also play into your decision.

Homeowner Involvement

When our bids came in we realized we weren't going to have the money we needed to build the house we wanted unless we found ways to cut costs. While we intended to build a similar house, our burned house had been built in 1972 and needed some updating. Those updates would amount to a greater cost than we were allowed under our policy, and we had to come up with some strategies to keep the costs down.

Admittedly, this wouldn't work for everybody because many people have full-time jobs which they have to do during their recovery. We are retired, so we had the time to dedicate to the task at hand. And while it might be a bit more difficult, those who are still working could employ some of the strategies in their non-working hours. We basically saw this as "going back to full-time work" while we were rebuilding in order to "earn back" the policy money we had been paying for over the years of home ownership.

Our contractor was willing to work with us, provided we kept to his schedule and didn't slow him down. Saying that, he would let us know ahead of time when the lights would be hung, the floor would be laid, the plumbing fixtures would be placed, etc. He gave us a budget and we took it as a challenge to come in under his budget so that we could add some things in other parts of the house that we wanted. So we became intimately acquainted with *ReStore*—the *Habitat for Humanity* stores where you can purchase all types of building materials at very little cost. For instance, we had a $3000 budget for lighting fixtures. We went to *ReStore* and found most of what we needed for under $1000. The rest we bought through an online building outlet called *Build.com*, thus saving ourselves $2000 to apply somewhere else. We bought our plumbing fixtures (toilets, bathtub and sinks, as well as faucets) at *ReStore*. We bought all our door knobs/handles at $2 a set, $3 for locking sets, still brand new in the box. Comparable prices in the stores were $20 and more per set. All of the electrical and plumbing items sold at *ReStore* have to meet current building code requirements, so for instance, the toilets all had low-water-use tanks.

**ReStore was the source of many
of our fixtures**

What we didn't find at *ReStore* and *Build.com*, we found at discount tile and flooring stores. We bought most of our doors through a big-box store which was offering discounts to fire victims. Some of the doors were specialty doors which we found at estate sales. We found an online stained glass company which fabricated a few panes of glass designed by my husband at very reasonable cost.

In this way, we were able to save a lot of money, have the extras we wanted and still stay close to our budget. We did dip into our content money which I covered in the "Contents" section of this book. As the contractor completed portions of the work he would submit a bill to us and we would take it to the credit union which held our mortgage and they would send the check. Overall, it was a smooth process and the house was completed pretty close to schedule and budget.

If you don't have the time to dedicate to searching out components for your home, all is not lost. Most contractors have a supplier who offers a variety of products in a wide range of prices. You will have to choose carefully, perhaps choosing higher-end floors and lower end fixtures, etc. The choice is yours and only you can decide what is most important to you.

Rebuilding Checklist

- ☐ **Demolition**
- ☐ **Tract Builder**
- ☐ **Self-contract**
- ☐ **Online House Plans**
- ☐ **Choosing a Contractor**
    - o Interview potential contractors
    - o Decide how much personal involvement you will want
    - o Look for alternate sources for fixtures and other construction items

Landscaping

Knowing trees, I understand the meaning of patience.
Knowing grass, I can appreciate persistence.
Hal Borland

How you deal with landscaping will be dependent on what you had before the disaster and what you want to have when you have finished your restoration. Not all insurance policies cover a complete renewal of your landscaping, so be sure to ask your adjuster what is covered. Sometimes, the limit will be a percentage of your home coverage, sometimes it will be so much per tree or shrub up to a certain limit. Depending on the extent of the land around your home, you may have more than a lawn and a few trees to think about.

If you live in the country on a large parcel of land, your most urgent need may be to prevent erosion of the soil after fire or flooding. Please see Appendix 2 for sources of information on how to handle erosion.

Wattles for erosion control

The *Colorado State Forest Service* was a great help in getting seedling trees. Sometimes there are limits to the number of trees you can get from the Forest Service, but if you are getting them for windbreaks or erosion prevention, the number allowed may vary. The cost is minimal for getting trees but you generally have to order them several months in advance. Since restoration of your land will be an ongoing process, it is good to include trees and bushes from the Forest Service in your restoration.

If you have to reseed grasses, be sure to use local grasses rather than exotics because they will have a better chance of surviving. The local *Extension Office* at your County Headquarters should be able to steer you in the right direction.

Often after a disaster, local nurseries will offer discounts to homeowners seeking to replace plants and trees. Be sure to ask.

Since we live in a forested area, many area homeowners offered young trees from their properties to those of us who had lost our trees. This helped both donor and receiver because the donors needed to further mitigate their own properties in the event of future fires. If the trees are too large to dig up and move on your own, you can hire tree movers who use their scoops to prepare the planting hole on your property and then scoop up the tree from the donor property. They take the scoop of dirt from your property to fill in the hole on the donor property and there is little trace of the work.

Our son, James, pounded metal posts for the protective fencing around the young trees

We were blessed to have many friends and family who came to help us replant. My husband wanted to get started on that part of our recovery because of the time it takes to grow a tree. One word of caution, however; if you are not living on or close to your property during the rebuild, don't be too hasty about planting. Young trees need lots of tender loving care, and they can't go without water when first planted.

Unloading trees for planting

Family members and friends planting aspen

An organization in our locale that did so much good and provided invaluable help to the residents of our forested area was *Black Forest Together*. While they didn't cut down black trees, their volunteers worked tirelessly to chip branches, do post-fire erosion control and replanting. They put up fences where needed and did a variety of other jobs. They also sponsored seedling tree distribution to provide a way for homeowners to begin to restore vegetation to their scorched lands. *Black Forest Together* also coordinated with the Air Force Academy for cadets to help in the cleanup effort and distributed *Walmart* gift cards to each family that was affected by the fire. This organization continues to help residents restore their property and works on fire mitigation projects as well.

Advance Preparation

Remember; when disaster strikes,
the time to prepare has passed.
Steven Cyros

Below are suggestions of things you can do before disaster strikes. Most people won't face a total loss, but if you think about it, many parts of the country are vulnerable to some sort of weather-related disaster. There are hurricanes and flooding in the Southeast and all up the Eastern Seaboard. There are tornadoes and flooding in the Midwest. There are fires in the mountains and earthquakes (which are not weather-related) in California. Winter can wreak havoc on the Northern states, causing power outages and food shortages. So, wherever you are, you should be prepared for a disruption in your life.

Home Inventory

There are a number of things we should have done beforehand that we hadn't thought of. One of the most important things was a home inventory which every home owner ought to have. A home inventory can be created in a number of ways. At the very least, take pictures of every room in the house, open every closet and cabinet and take a picture. Open every drawer and take a picture. Save those pictures in "the Cloud' or on an external digital storage device, or make a hard copy and give it to somebody in your family to keep for you. You could also put it in a safe deposit box at your bank. Another way to inventory your home is to use the inventory list I have included as Appendix 8. You can use it to go through every room in your house and check off all the items you have in your home. After completing it, make a copy of it and save it as you would your pictures. You should also scan it and save it in "The Cloud" or on an external storage device. If you depend on an external storage device, do not store it in your home where it might get destroyed in a fire or flood!

Do not depend on a fire-proof strong box to protect your valuable papers. All the papers in our strong box were charred beyond recognition due to the intense heat, and the silver was melted.

"Fire-proof" strong box

Valuable Documents

Make copies of all your important certificates, passports, social security card, certificates of deposit, credit cards, financial records, etc. These copies, like the home inventory, can be either digital or hard copies, and they should be stored away from your property or in "The Cloud."

Pictures and other Memorabilia

If you have copies of your pictures in digital files, you can store them in "The Cloud" or on an external storage device. If you only have paper copies, keep them together in a place where you could easily grab them if you have to leave your home quickly. Keep in mind that this wouldn't work if you were away when the order to evacuate came. So it is a good idea to save as much as you can away from your home—either digitally, with a family member or in a safe deposit box.

Emergency Supplies

Sometimes before a disaster hits there are advance warnings. The weather service often tracks hurricanes and other storms and issues warnings for people to be prepared to evacuate. In some locations of the Midwest, tornadoes are a fact of life during the summer months and so the possibility of one hitting a particular area is always real. In our case, we were being warned of the fire danger due to lack of moisture. In the event you have a chance to grab a few items on your way out, it is a good idea to have an emergency kit prepared in advance. I have listed recommended items to have in such a kit in Appendix 9.

You may think of other items to include. Again, it is important to have the kit prepared and to have it in a location where you can easily access it on your way out. In addition, **make a list of the things to grab if you have to leave quickly.** When you are in the midst of an emergency, you won't always think of specific items you might want to have, so a list, readily available, would be very helpful.

Review your Insurance Coverage

Insurance companies recommend that you review your homeowner's policy at least once a year. You may have made some upgrades or changes to your home or property which should be taken into account for insurance purposes. You may have added a shed, barn, deck or other outbuilding. It is also important to think about any valuables which you might have which may need to be put under a separate rider or policy; such as silver or gold, collections such as baseball cards, stamps or coins, musical instruments, fine art, etc. You also want to insure trailers, campers, recreational vehicles and all your cars. Vehicles will not be covered under a homeowner's policy but will require their own policy.

Also remember that if you have any livestock, you may want to insure it under a livestock policy. Losses for livestock are generally not covered under a homeowner's policy.

Advance Preparation Checklist

☐ **Home Inventory**
☐ **Valuable Documents**
☐ **Pictures and other Memorabilia**
☐ **Emergency Supplies**
☐ **Review Insurance Coverage**

You Can Survive a Disaster

Always forward, never back
St. Junipero Serra

Keep in mind that even after a devastating loss, you can recover and move forward. It isn't easy, but it is possible. Help is available if you seek it out.

Casa Colorada

We have learned a lot about ourselves and how to deal with unplanned events in our life. About ourselves we learned that we were able to cope with the hand we were dealt when the fire hit. We worked together closely for the year of our rebuild and in the words of St. Junipero Serra, were able to keep moving "always forward, never back." We saw how a family can pull together in a crisis and will always be grateful to our children, their spouses, our grandchildren, our siblings and friends who came from various states to lend a hand and to offer moral support. There was a lot of problem solving which had to be done on the spot in order not to hold up progress, and we learned to be confident in the decisions we were making on a daily basis.

Losing all our earthly possessions was not the end of the world for us, but it did facilitate our thinking about what was truly important. We have learned detachment from material things, and are trying not to become attached to the new things we have purchased. After going to countless estate sales, we became aware of how much junk people store for decades. Those items just deteriorate and take up space. In addition, when we simply store furniture, dishes, clothing and other articles that we don't use, we are depriving their use to somebody who would benefit from them. We resolved not to fill every nook and cranny of our new home and after we moved in, we made a rule that anytime we brought something in, we would have to remove something so as not to accumulate too much. It has also meant that we evaluate every purchase and think twice before buying things.

We are very sad to have lost memorabilia and pictures which can't be replaced, but we have come to accept that reality. Family and friends were very kind to send us pictures and to share a few precious possessions with us. Beyond that, we have the memories.

Our life is simpler now, and we consider that a positive result of what we went through. We knew that at some point we would have to sort everything we owned and discard much of it. While a natural disaster is not something one would wish to endure, it doesn't have to inhibit us from continuing to live a fulfilling life. If anything, it shows us just what is most important, and that has nothing to do with the items we own.

Gratitude

We must find time to stop and thank the people
who make a difference in our lives.
John F. Kennedy

I would be remiss if I didn't recall with gratitude all the help, love, prayers and kindnesses extended to us during the trying times after the fire. Listed below are the people and organizations we want to thank. Hopefully, nobody has been left out, but if that has happened, please know it wasn't intentional.

- Our sons Ian, James and Michael, our daughter Rebekah and our daughters-in-law Paula and Breánne

- Our siblings and their spouses: Ben and Eleanor Gastellum, Ed and Carolyn Gastellum, Richard Gastellum and Kelly Collins, Steve and Karman and our Godson Dan Gastellum, Barbara Martin, John and Marie Martin, Ed Rutherford and Gloria Thomas

- Our Friends: John and Peggy Ocken, Karl and Sharon Keas, Laura Guiang, George and Helene Forster and Armond and Pat Ipri

- Friends from the Parish of Immaculate Conception who helped us clean up the mess, provided meals, planted trees and held a clothing shower for me

- Mary Trionfera and the parishioners of St. Joseph Catholic Church in Fort Collins, CO, who generously held a shower on our behalf

- The Parish of St. Gabriel in Colorado Springs which held a shower for us to supply our new home with much needed household items

- Andrea Curran who restored the statue of the Blessed Virgin Mary

- My brother Ben and sister-in-law Eleanor, and my son, Ian, who patiently read over this manuscript and made helpful corrections and suggestions

- Terri Gray and Catholic Charities of Southern Colorado

- Southern Baptist Disaster Relief

- Church of Christ Disaster Relief

- Salvation Army

- Samaritan's Purse

- Black Forest Together

- Michael Richardson from Enservio who taught us how to list our contents.
  http://www.enservio.com/

- My husband Larry who encouraged me to write this book and helped me at every step along the way

- And most of all....*Deo Gratias*

Appendix 1, Definitions

Actual Cash Value (ACV)

The actual cash value in a homeowner's insurance policy is the cost of repairing or replacing a home at the time of loss with depreciation considered. Most standard homeowner's insurance policies cover the replacement cost of your home's physical structure and the actual cash value of the insured's personal property. An insurance policy with coverage based on actual cash value is the least expensive to purchase, since depreciation is considered and the claim payments are generally lower. The ACV cannot exceed the limits laid out in the policy.

Additional Coverage

Additional coverage can be purchased to provide protection for events or coverage not included in the basic homeowner's policy. For instance, some policies don't cover wind damage. You can buy coverage for that. If you have particularly valuable items, they should be insured separately because the homeowner's policy won't pay their value if they are lost or damaged. Such additional coverage is called a "rider" or an "endorsement."

Adjuster

The person paid by the insurance company to investigate your loss and settle your claim.

Agent

The insurance company representative who is licensed by the state to sell insurance and negotiate contracts for the company. This is not the person who handles your claim.

Antique

An antique is a collectable object which is at least 100 years old. It can be a piece of furniture, a piece of art, pottery, implement, article of clothing or anything else, so long as it is 100 or more years old.

Claim

The request made by the insured for payment of the benefits outlined in the insurance policy.

Contents

All of the items found in a home. For insurance purposes, built-in fixtures such as those found in a bathroom, as well as built-in ranges, light fixtures, etc., are not considered as contents and wouldn't be covered in the contents or personal property part of the claim. Such built-in items would be covered under construction costs.

Coverage

The amount of protection provided by an insurance policy.

Depreciation

Depreciation is the decrease in the value of property or contents due to age, use or obsolescence. Insurers tend to calculate depreciation differently but an easy way to determine depreciation is to consider the expected lifetime of an item, then subtract a percentage of value for each year since its purchase. For example, say you bought a gaming system for $1,000 four years ago that is expected to last 10 years. The estimated depreciation calculation would be 1,000 / 10 x 4, which equals $400. This leaves the actual cash value of the gaming system which is covered by your home owner's policy to be $600 ($1,000 - $400).

Exclusion

Specific condition or circumstance listed in the homeowner's policy as not being covered under the policy. Flooding is an exclusion usually listed in a homeowner's policy.

Guaranteed or Extended Replacement Cost

This option offers the most protection and is the most expensive. The extended replacement cost option pays up to a certain percentage above the cost to rebuild a home, between 20 and 25%, even if the cost exceeds the estimated value of the home. The primary purpose of the option is to protect the policyholder against sudden increases in materials or construction costs which can occur when many claims in an area are made.

Loss of Use Coverage

Loss of use coverage is a rider on your homeowner's policy which covers the cost of your rent and possibly other living expenses after a covered loss during the time it takes to repair or rebuild your home.

Market Value

The price something would sell for in the current market.

Personal Property

All tangible property not considered as real property. The typical homeowner's policy will have a limit on the amount it will pay for personal property lost in a fire or other disaster.

Real Property

Land, homes, outbuildings, vegetation

Replacement Cost Coverage (RCC)

The replacement cost for homeowners insurance is the amount of money it would take to replace your damaged or destroyed home with the exact same or a similar home in today's market, without taking into account depreciation.

This is the value of the home minus the land it sits on. An appraiser determines the value of the home's construction materials, any exceptional or valuable upgrades in fixtures or added living space (porch, entertainment space, decks, etc.) and determines your house's value. For a simple example, say you purchased a new home for $400,000. That price likely included the cost of the lot it was built on and the cost of constructing the dwelling. If the lot was priced at $50,000 you only need to insure the cost of the home, which would be $350,000.

The replacement or rebuild cost is usually paid in installments. First, the insurer will give the homeowner a check to get the rebuild started. As progress is made and the building continues, the insurer will pay out as needed until the project is complete up to the total replacement cost allowed under the policy. Upgrades and extras in the new house are generally not covered as part of replacement costs because they were not present in the original house.

It is important to review your policy annually with your agent to make sure that your policy is providing you with adequate coverage. Inflation can quickly depreciate the value of your home and if you aren't properly insured, you might not get the amount needed to rebuild. Also, if you make improvements to your home, your agent should take that into account in figuring the coverage for your home.

Rider
An add-on to your policy which provides coverage for specific services or items not covered under your standard homeowner's policy. Riders incur an additional, but usually minimal, cost.

Vintage
A collectable item which is generally over 50 years old. Some items can be considered vintage if they are less than 50 years old because nothing of the kind existed more than 50 years ago, such as a particular video game. They can also be considered vintage if they were of a collectable nature but are no longer being manufactured, such as certain Disney items or toys, etc.

Appendix 2, List of Resources

Much of the information for this book was gleaned from a number of sources. They are noted below:

Antique Valuation
https://antiques.lovetoknow.com/Antique_Furniture_Value_Lookup

Erosion Control
http://extension.colostate.edu/soil-erosion-control-after-wildfire-6-308/

Estate Sales
www.estatesales.net

FEMA Information
http://ohp.parks.ca.gov/?page_id=25506

Federal Reserve Bank Locations
https://www.federalreserve.gov/aboutthefed/federal-reserve-system.htm

Flood Information
https://www.ready.gov/floods

House Plans
https://www.houseplans.com/

http://www.homeplans.com/

Insurance Terms

http://www.helpinsure.com/home/cpmhomeglossary.html

Receipt organization programs and Apps

Neat https://www.neat.com/solutions/document-retention-organization/

Evernote https://www.makeuseof.com/tag/how-to-use-evernote-the-missing-manual-full-text/

Shoeboxed https://www.shoeboxed.com/

Removing Drywall after a Flood

https://www.popularmechanics.com/home/interior-projects/how-to/a8242/removing-so
ggy-drywall-in-8-not-so-easy-steps-14261117/

Salvaging Photographs

https://www.thoughtco.com/salvaging-flood-and-water-damaged-photos-1422276

Sample Forms for processing claims

https://www.uphelp.org/guide/contents-claim-help

Stained Glass Windows, Custom

http://www.stainedglasswindows.com/

U.S. Forest Service, Restoring the land after a fire

https://www.nrcs.usda.gov/wps/portal/nrcs/detail/wa/ho
me/?cid=STELPRDB1259629

Vegetative Recovery after a Fire will vary depending on location:

Colorado:
https://dspace.library.colostate.edu/bitstream/handle/102 17/183665/AEXT_ucsu20622 63072002.pdf?sequence=2&isAllowed=y

California:
https://www.cnps.org/wp-content/uploads/2018/04/CNPS-fire-recovery-guide-LR-040618.pdf

In other states, please check with your State Forest Service

Appendix 3, Support Agencies

American Red Cross Disaster Relief
http://www.redcross.org/about-us/our-work/disaster-relief

Catholic Charities Disaster Response
https://catholiccharitiesusa.org/find-help

Church of Christ Disaster Response Team
https://www.churchesofchristdrt.org/

Church of the Nazarene Disaster Response
http://www.usacanadaregion.org/ministries/compassionate-ministries/nazarene-disaster
-response

Goodwill Industries
http://www.goodwill.org/?s=store+locator

Salvation Army Disaster Relief
https://disaster.salvationarmyusa.org/aboutus/?ourservices

Samaritan's Purse Disaster Relief
https://www.samaritanspurse.org/what-we-do/crisis-and-disaster-response/

Southern Baptist Disaster Relief
https://www.namb.net/send-relief/disaster-relief

Appendix 4, Things to Look for First

- ☐ Financial Records
- ☐ Certificates
- ☐ Family Records
- ☐ Precious Metals
- ☐ Coins
- ☐ Jewelry
- ☐ Sterling Silver Flatware
- ☐ Photographs
- ☐ Computers
- ☐ External Hard Drive
- ☐ Cash

Appendix 5, Questions for a Potential Contractor

- ☐ How long have you been in business?
- ☐ Do you have any special expertise or training in the building trades?
- ☐ How soon are you available to start my house?
- ☐ How long do you think it will take to finish my house?
- ☐ Will you be supervising the project, or will you have an on-site foreman?
- ☐ Do you have employees or do you use subcontractors?
- ☐ Are you fully insured for injury and liability? To what limit?
- ☐ How many projects similar to this one have you completed in the last year?
- ☐ Would you furnish me with a list of those projects so that I can go see them?
- ☐ Would you furnish me with a list of referrals?
- ☐ Are you willing to work with me in procuring some of the supplies for the project?
- ☐ Do you have any objections to my visiting the jobsite while work is in progress?
- ☐ Are you registered with the BBB?
- ☐ What kind of a warranty do you offer?
- ☐ Who handles warranty work?

Appendix 6, How to Replace Documents

Birth/Death Records

Contact the Vital Records Department of your County.

Citizenship Records

https://www.uscis.gov/n-565

Driver's License

Contact your local Department of Motor Vehicles.

Income Tax Records

https://www.irs.gov/newsroom/how-to-get-a-copy-of-your-prior-years-tax-information

Insurance Records

Contact your insurance companies for copies of your policies.

Marriage/Divorce Certificate:

Contact the Vital Records Department of the County where the marriage or divorce took place.

Medical Records

Contact your doctors directly for copies. You may have to pay by the page for these records.

Military Medals

https://www.archives.gov/veterans/replace-medals.html

Military Records

https://www.archives.gov/veterans/military-service-records

Passports

Fill out Form DS-64 available at
https://eforms.state.gov/Forms/ds64.pdf and mail it to
the address on the form. Then have a passport photo
taken at Walgreens or Costco, UPS store, or any number
of places and then go to the post office with proof of
citizenship and your identity, fill out the appropriate
application form and pay your fee. The purpose of the
above form is to report the loss of the passport so that
you can be issued another.

Property Title Certificate

Contact your local County Recording Office.

Social Security Cards

https://www.ssa.gov/ssnumber/

Will or Trust

Contact the lawyer who prepared it.

Appendix 7, Damaged Money

If your loss is due to fire, you may be dealing with burnt paper money and fire damaged coins.

Paper Money

Paper money will be brittle, so be very careful with it and wrap it in plastic to preserve it. If half or more of each bill remains intact, you can take it to a regional Federal Reserve Bank for replacement. (See Appendix 4 for a list of Federal Reserve Banks). If there isn't a Federal Reserve Bank near you, you can mail the money using registered mail, return receipt requested to:

Department of the Treasury
Bureau of Engraving and Printing
Office of Currency Standards
P.O. Box 37048
Washington, DC 20013

Coins

Damaged or melted coins may also be taken to your regional Federal Reserve Bank or they can be mailed the same way as paper money to:

Superintendent U.S. Mint
P.O. Box 400
Philadelphia, PA 19105

Savings Bonds

If you have U.S. Savings Bonds that are destroyed, use form PD-F-1048 (1) which you can get from your bank or online at www.ustreas.gov and mail to:

Department of the Treasury Bureau of the Public Debt
Savings Bonds Operations
P.O. Box 1328
Parkersburg, WV 26106-1328

Appendix 8, Home Inventory Checklist

Inside the House

This checklist is arranged by room. While it may not include everything single item, it is very complete. Items that are installed, like a wall oven or medicine cabinets, light fixtures, plumbing fixtures, etc., are not covered as contents, but come out of the money used to rebuild the house, so they are not listed here. Use this list to go through each room of your house and check the items you have now. Then, as with your other important documents, save a copy of it safely away from your house (in a safe-deposit box, with a child or friend, or in the "Cloud.")

Attic

- ☐ Furniture
- ☐ Memorabilia
- ☐ Trunks
- ☐ Clothes

Bathroom 1

- ☐ Cleaning Supplies
- ☐ Cosmetics
- ☐ Hamper
- ☐ Rug

- ☐ Shower Curtain/Rod
- ☐ Soap
- ☐ Soap Dish
- ☐ Towels
- ☐ Tissue Holder
- ☐ Toilet Tissue Holder
- ☐ Window Covering

Bathroom 2

- ☐ Cleaning Supplies
- ☐ Cosmetics
- ☐ Hamper
- ☐ Rug
- ☐ Shower Curtain/Rod
- ☐ Soap
- ☐ Soap Dish
- ☐ Towels
- ☐ Tissue Holder
- ☐ Toilet Tissue Holder
- ☐ Window Covering

Bathroom 3

- ☐ Cleaning Supplies
- ☐ Cosmetics
- ☐ Hamper
- ☐ Rug
- ☐ Shower Curtain/Rod
- ☐ Soap
- ☐ Soap Dish
- ☐ Towels
- ☐ Tissue Holder
- ☐ Toilet Tissue Holder

☐ Window Covering

Bathroom 4
☐ Cleaning Supplies
☐ Cosmetics
☐ Hamper
☐ Rug
☐ Shower Curtain/Rod
☐ Soap
☐ Soap Dish
☐ Towels
☐ Tissue Holder
☐ Toilet Tissue Holder
☐ Window Covering

Bedroom 1, Master
☐ Bed
  o Bed Frame
  o Bedspread or Comforter
  o Blanket
  o Bottom Sheet
  o Box Spring
  o Mattress
  o Mattress Cover
  o Pillows
  o Pillow Cases
  o Top Sheet
☐ Bedside Table
☐ Bedside Lamp
☐ Blanket Chest
☐ Chair
☐ Clock

☐ Clothing (see page 136 for detailed list)
☐ Closet Storage Containers
☐ Dresser
☐ Hangers
☐ Radio
☐ Rugs
☐ Television
☐ Valet
☐ Window Coverings

Bedroom 2

☐ Bed
  o Bed Frame
  o Bedspread or Comforter
  o Blanket
  o Bottom Sheet
  o Box Spring
  o Mattress
  o Mattress Cover
  o Pillows
  o Pillow Cases
  o Top Sheet
☐ Bedside Table
☐ Bedside Lamp
☐ Blanket Chest
☐ Chair
☐ Clock
☐ Clothing (see page 136 for detailed list)
☐ Closet Storage Containers
☐ Dresser
☐ Hangers
☐ Radio

- ☐ Rugs
- ☐ Television
- ☐ Valet
- ☐ Window Coverings

Bedroom 3

- ☐ Bed
  - o Bed Frame
  - o Bedspread or Comforter
  - o Blanket
  - o Bottom Sheet
  - o Box Spring
  - o Mattress
  - o Mattress Cover
  - o Pillows
  - o Pillow Cases
  - o Top Sheet
- ☐ Bedside Table
- ☐ Bedside Lamp
- ☐ Blanket Chest
- ☐ Chair
- ☐ Clock
- ☐ Clothing (see page 136 for detailed list)
- ☐ Closet Storage Containers
- ☐ Dresser
- ☐ Hangers
- ☐ Radio
- ☐ Rugs
- ☐ Television
- ☐ Valet
- ☐ Window Coverings

Bedroom 4

- ☐ Bed
  - o Bed Frame
  - o Bedspread or Comforter
  - o Blanket
  - o Bottom Sheet
  - o Box Spring
  - o Mattress
  - o Mattress Cover
  - o Pillows
  - o Pillow Cases
  - o Top Sheet
- ☐ Bedside Table
- ☐ Bedside Lamp
- ☐ Blanket Chest
- ☐ Chair
- ☐ Clock
- ☐ Clothing (see page 136 for detailed list)
- ☐ Closet Storage Containers
- ☐ Dresser
- ☐ Hangers
- ☐ Radio
- ☐ Rugs
- ☐ Television
- ☐ Valet
- ☐ Window Coverings

Bedroom 5

- ☐ Bed
  - o Bed Frame
  - o Bedspread or Comforter

- o Blanket
- o Bottom Sheet
- o Box Spring
- o Mattress
- o Mattress Cover
- o Pillows
- o Pillow Cases
- o Top Sheet
- ☐ Bedside Table
- ☐ Bedside Lamp
- ☐ Blanket Chest
- ☐ Chair
- ☐ Clock
- ☐ Clothing (see page 136 for detailed list)
- ☐ Closet Storage Containers
- ☐ Dresser
- ☐ Hangers
- ☐ Radio
- ☐ Rugs
- ☐ Valet
- ☐ Window Coverings

Craft/Sewing Room

- ☐ Chair
- ☐ Craft Supplies
- ☐ Rug
- ☐ Sewing Machine
- ☐ Special Craft Equipment
- ☐ Storage Containers
- ☐ Table
- ☐ Window Coverings

Dining Room

- ☐ Buffet
- ☐ Chairs...how many?
- ☐ China Hutch
  - ○ China
  - ○ Bowls
  - ○ Cups
  - ○ Dessert Plates
  - ○ Dinner Plates
  - ○ Salad Plates
  - ○ Saucers
  - ○ Serving Bowls
  - ○ Serving Platters
  - ☐ Crystal/Glass
    - ○ Beer Glasses...how many?
    - ○ Cordial/Liqueur Glasses
    - ○ Highball Glasses...
    - ○ Irish Coffee Glasses
    - ○ Lowball Glasses
    - ○ Martini Glasses
    - ○ Water Glasses...
    - ○ Red Wine Glasses
    - ○ White Wine Glasses
- ☐ Rug
- ☐ Silverware
  - ○ Dinner Forks
  - ○ Knives
  - ○ Salad Forks
  - ○ Serving Pieces
  - ○ Soup Spoons
  - ○ Teaspoons
- ☐ Table
- ☐ Table Extensions

- ☐ Table Pad
- ☐ Window Coverings

Entry Way

- ☐ Bench or Chair
- ☐ Boots
- ☐ Coat Rack
- ☐ Coats
- ☐ Hats
- ☐ Hall tree
- ☐ Shoe Rack
- ☐ Shoes
- ☐ Table
- ☐ Umbrella

Kitchen

- ☐ Baking pans
- ☐ Casseroles
- ☐ Dishes
  - o Dinner Plates...how many?
  - o Salad Plates
  - o Bowls
  - o Cups
  - o Saucers
  - o Platters
  - o Serving Bowls
- ☐ Flatware
  - o Dinner Forks
  - o Salad Forks
  - o Knives
  - o Spoons
  - o Serving Spoons

- ☐ Extra Pieces
- ☐ Food
    - o Alcohol (wine, etc.)
    - o Baking Supplies
    - o Beverages
    - o Canned Goods
    - o Condiments
    - o Grains
    - o Nuts
    - o Oils
    - o Packaged Foods
    - o Spices
- ☐ Food Storage Containers
- ☐ Food Wrap
- ☐ Furniture
- ☐ Chairs...How many?
- ☐ Stools
- ☐ Rugs
- ☐ Table
- ☐ Knives
    - o Bread
    - o Butcher
    - o Carving
    - o Carving Fork
    - o Chefs
    - o Paring
    - o Steak
    - o Specialty Knives
- ☐ Linens
- ☐ Small Appliances
- ☐ Blender
- ☐ Coffee Pot

- ☐ Food Processor
- ☐ Juicer
- ☐ Kettle
- ☐ Microwave (if not built in)
- ☐ Stand Mixer
- ☐ Toaster
- ☐ Toaster Oven
- ☐ Pots and Pans
- ☐ Refrigerator and all its Contents
- ☐ Utensils
- ☐ Waffle Iron
- ☐ Window Coverings

Hallway

- ☐ Lamp
- ☐ Table
- ☐ Mirror
- ☐ Pictures
- ☐ Rug

Laundry Room

- ☐ Dryer
- ☐ Folding Table
- ☐ Hangers
- ☐ Hanging Rack
- ☐ Iron
- ☐ Ironing Board
- ☐ Washer

Library

- ☐ Book Shelves
- ☐ Books, how many?

- ☐ Chairs
- ☐ Collectible Books, how many? What kind?
- ☐ Lamp
- ☐ Rug
- ☐ Table
- ☐ Window Coverings

Living Room

- ☐ Coffee Table
- ☐ Couch
- ☐ Decorative Items
- ☐ End Tables
- ☐ Lamps
- ☐ Piano
- ☐ Rug
- ☐ Shelves
- ☐ Side Chairs
- ☐ Window Coverings

Man Cave

- ☐ Bar/Bar Equipment
- ☐ Electronic Equipment
- ☐ Lamps
- ☐ Recliners
- ☐ Refrigerator
- ☐ Rug
- ☐ Tables
- ☐ Television
- ☐ Window Coverings

Mudroom

- ☐ Bench

- ☐ Cabinets
- ☐ Rug
- ☐ Shoe Rack
- ☐ Window Coverings

Office

- ☐ Chair
- ☐ Computer
- ☐ Desk
- ☐ Desk Contents
- ☐ Filing Cabinets
- ☐ Lamp
- ☐ Office Supplies
- ☐ Printer
- ☐ Scanner
- ☐ Table
- ☐ Window Coverings

Rec Room

- ☐ Audio/Visual Equipment
- ☐ Board Games
- ☐ Chairs
- ☐ Couch
- ☐ Electronic/Gaming Equipment
- ☐ Entertainment/Media Center
- ☐ Lamps
- ☐ Rug
- ☐ Table

Clothing

Children's

- ☐ Athletic Clothes
- ☐ Dresses
- ☐ Jeans
- ☐ Pants
- ☐ Socks
- ☐ Shoes
- ☐ Shirts
- ☐ Shorts
- ☐ Skirts
- ☐ Swimsuit
- ☐ Underwear

Men's

- ☐ Athletic Clothes
- ☐ Belts
- ☐ Dress Shirts
- ☐ Formal Wear
- ☐ Jeans
- ☐ Polo Shirts
- ☐ Shoes... how many? What kind?
- ☐ Shorts
- ☐ Slacks
- ☐ Socks
- ☐ Swimming Trunks
- ☐ Ties
- ☐ T-shirts
- ☐ Undershirts

☐ Undershorts

Women's

☐ Athletic Wear
☐ Blouses
☐ Bras
☐ Camisoles
☐ Dresses
☐ Formal Wear
☐ Shoes...how many? What kind?
☐ Shirts
☐ Shorts
☐ Skirts
☐ Slacks
☐ Slips
☐ Socks
☐ Stockings
☐ Swimsuit
☐ Underwear

Linens

Bathroom

☐ Bath Mats
☐ Bath Towels
☐ Face Cloths
☐ Hand Towels

Bedroom

☐ Bedspreads
☐ Blankets

- ☐ Bottom Sheets
- ☐ Comforters
- ☐ Mattress Covers
- ☐ Pillows
- ☐ Pillow Cases
- ☐ Top Sheets

Kitchen

- ☐ Dish Cloths
- ☐ Hand Towels
- ☐ Napkins
- ☐ Place Mats
- ☐ Pot Holders
- ☐ Table
- ☐ Table Cloths
- ☐ Table Runners

Specialized Items

- ☐ Antiques
- ☐ Antique Clocks
- ☐ Cameras
- ☐ Climate Control Appliances
- ☐ Collections (stamp, coin, etc.)
- ☐ Decorative Items
- ☐ Dehumidifier
- ☐ Fans
- ☐ Fine Art
- ☐ Fireplace Equipment
- ☐ Jewelry
- ☐ Musical Instruments
- ☐ Pet Supplies

- ☐ Portable Heaters
- ☐ Sheet Music
- ☐ Shelving
- ☐ Sump Pump
- ☐ Toys

Outside the House

Deck or Patio

- ☐ Chairs...how many?
- ☐ Cushions
- ☐ Deck Cover
- ☐ Dining Table
- ☐ Floor Covering
- ☐ Grill
- ☐ Grill Cover
- ☐ Deck Lighting
- ☐ Roller Shades
- ☐ Side Tables
- ☐ Umbrellas

Garage

- ☐ Bicycles
- ☐ Christmas and Other Holiday Decorations
- ☐ Freezer and all its Contents
- ☐ Hand Tools
- ☐ Power Tools
- ☐ Shelving
- ☐ Sports Equipment
- ☐ Storage Boxes/Contents

☐ Work Bench

Shed

☐ Axe
☐ Flower Pots
☐ Gardening Supplies
☐ Hoe
☐ Hoses
☐ Lawn Mower
☐ Rake
☐ Shovel
☐ Snow Shovel
☐ Weed Wacker
☐ Other Tools

Barn

What you keep in a barn is an individual thing. If you have horses, you will need to inventory your tack, feed and all supplies for your animals. Livestock have their own specialized equipment, which again, you will need to list and inventory. In addition:

☐ Animal Carriers
☐ Buckets
☐ Feed Storage
☐ Feed Troughs
☐ Grain/Hay
☐ Medications
☐ Snow Blower
☐ Tractor
☐ Wagons
☐ Water Troughs

☐ Wheelbarrow

Shop

☐ Bench Grinder
☐ Drills
☐ Hand Tools
☐ Ladder
☐ Paint
☐ Paint Supplies
☐ Power Saw
☐ Sanders
☐ Saw horse
☐ Stool
☐ Storage Cabinets
☐ Tool Storage Cabinet
☐ Workbench

Appendix 9, Emergency Supplies

- ☐ Blankets/Sleeping Bags
- ☐ Can opener (manual)
- ☐ Cell phone
- ☐ Cell phone cable to connect to charger
- ☐ Cell phone charger--solar or hand cranked as you may be without electricity
- ☐ Comfort items for children such as blankets, stuffed animals, books, etc.
- ☐ Copy of your homeowner's insurance policy
- ☐ Duct tape
- ☐ Extra batteries for radio
- ☐ Eye glasses
- ☐ Fire extinguisher
- ☐ First-Aid kit
- ☐ Food in sealed containers
- ☐ Hand-crank, solar or battery powered radio
- ☐ LED Flashlights or headlamps. LED lights don't use as much battery power as conventional flashlights
- ☐ List of important phone numbers in case your cell phone is lost or battery is dead
- ☐ Matches or lighters
- ☐ Medications
- ☐ Plastic bags
- ☐ Pocket knife
- ☐ Road maps--don't depend solely on cell phones and GPS devices

- ☐ Sanitary supplies
- ☐ Shovel
- ☐ Tarp or sheet plastic
- ☐ Toilet paper
- ☐ Tools
- ☐ Water--one gallon per person per day x 7 days
- ☐ Water purification tablets

Appendix 10, One Final List

This, your final list, is to check off as you accomplish your recovery. With so many things to do seemingly all at once, it is good to have a checklist to make sure you are on track with the big picture.

- ☐ **Notify Family and Friends**
- ☐ **Meet with your Adjuster**
- ☐ **Attend to Temporary Housing**
- ☐ **Secure Remaining Possessions**
- ☐ **Hunt for Treasure**
- ☐ **See to Utilities**
  - o Telephone
  - o Water and sewer
  - o Electricity
  - o Natural gas
  - o Cable television
- ☐ **Acquire the Tools You Need for Your Clean-up**
- ☐ **Portable Toilet (if needed)**
- ☐ **Sun Protection/Shelter**
- ☐ **Chairs and Tables**
- ☐ **Storage Unit**
- ☐ **Shed**
- ☐ **Recycle Materials**
  - o Metals
  - o Precious Metals
  - o Stone or Bricks

- **Get help**
  - Government Agencies
  - Churches
  - Non-profit Agencies
  - Mental Health
  - Animals
- **Flooding**
  - Water
  - Documents
  - Photographs
  - Cleaning up
  - Removing Debris
  - Rugs/Carpets/Upholstered Furniture
  - Other Furniture
  - Mold
  - Food
  - Medicine
  - Before Moving In
- **Insurance details**
  - Coverage for Property
  - Coverage for Loss of Use
  - Coverage for Miscellaneous Expenses
  - Coverage for Livestock
  - Coverage for Automobiles and other Vehicles
  - Receipts
- **Contents**
- **Replacing Household Goods**
- **Rebuilding**
- **Choosing a Contractor**
- **Landscaping**
- **Advance Preparation**
  - Home Inventory

o Valuable Documents
o Pictures and other Memorabilia
o Emergency Supplies
o Review your Insurance Policy
☐ **MOVE IN AND ENJOY YOUR NEW HOME!**

Credits

Giving credit where credit is due is a very rewarding habit to form. Its rewards are inestimable.
Loretta Young

P. 2
Shaking Hands
Photo by Lucas [Public domain], from Wikimedia Commons

P. 15
Septic Truck
Photo by Dwight Burdette
(https://commons.wikimedia.org/wiki?File.Septage_pump_truck_Highland_Michigan.JPG),
https://creativecommons.org/licenses/by/3.0/legalcode

P. 16
Satellite Dish
By Loadmaster (David R. Tribble) This image was made by Loadmaster (David R. Tribble)
(https://creativecommons.org/licenses/by-sa/3.0) or
GFDL (http://www.gnu.org/copyleft/fdl.html)], from Wikimedia Commons

P. 31
Catholic Charities
Photo by George Armstrong (This image is from the FEMA Photo Library.) [Public domain], via Wikimedia Commons

P. 31
Southern Baptist Relief
Photo by Mark Wolfe (This image is from the FEMA Photo Library.) [Public domain], via Wikimedia Commons

P. 34
Sherriff's Deputy rescuing horses
Photo by Jerilee Bennett/The Gazette, Colorado Springs, CO, June 12, 2013, with permission

P. 41
Missouri flood cleanup
Photo by Andrea Booher (This image is from the FEMA Photo Library.) [Public domain], via Wikimedia Commons

P. 42
Cleaning up flooding damage in Minnesota
Photo by Patsy Lynch (This image is from the FEMA Photo Library.) [Public domain], via Wikimedia Commons

P. 43
Mold on ceiling
By Infrogmation [GFDL (http://www.gnu.org/copyleft/fdl.html), CC BY 2.0 (https://creativecommons.org/licenses/by/2.0), CC BY 2.5 (https://creativecommons.org/licenses/by/2.5) or CC BY 3.0 (https://creativecommons.org/licenses/by/3.0)], from Wikimedia Commons

P. 45
Evacuating flood victims in Missouri, 2008
By John Shea (This image is from the FEMA Photo Library.) [Public domain], via Wikimedia Commons

Some of the family pictures were taken by my brother Steve
and my sister-in-law Karman Gastellum.

The remaining photos were taken by me with a cell phone, and
the resolution is not of the highest quality. However, I have
included those pictures because they help to tell the story.

*So comes snow after fire, and even dragons have their
endings*
J.R.R. Tolkien, **The Hobbit**

About the Author

We must let go of the life we have planned, so as to accept the one that is waiting for us.
Joseph Campbell

In 2013, Fran was vacationing with her husband in Alaska when the worst fire in Colorado history incinerated their home and all of their possessions.

Five years later, she completed **Rising from the Ashes** which chronicles their recovery and also gives many helpful suggestions for others going through a similar experience. She believes that you can suffer a disaster of this magnitude, work your way through the grief and move forward to restore your life. On the way, you can discover strengths and abilities you may not have known you had, and you can enjoy what lies ahead.

Fran Rutherford has been married to her husband Larry for 48 years, is the mother of five children and grandmother of 17. The daughter of a National Park Service employee, she was fortunate to live in some of the Nation's most beautiful places, particularly Yellowstone National Park. After marrying, she and her husband lived in many wonderful Air Force locations in the US as well as in Germany and England. She has written study guides for students and teachers of Classical history and literature and enjoys spending time with family, traveling, reading, writing and hiking.